Anatomy Of A Barber

The Hair Professionals Guide To Success

by Al Reid, aka Alsmillions

Published by FastPencil

Published by FastPencil
307 Orchard City Drive
Suite 210
Campbell CA 95008 USA
info@fastpencil.com
(408) 540-7571
(408) 540-7572 (Fax)
http://www.fastpencil.com

Printed in the United States of America.

First Edition

To my wife Karima, for your undying support. I love you honey.

To Bessie Reid, "Mama Bessie" for raising me to be a man and giving me the best you knew how to give. I will never forget your sacrifices. RIP mom.

To Alvin G. Reid, lll, Calvin J. Reid, Maxwell K. Reid and Jordan G. Reid. I love you and I hope you will build on what I've started. Much success to all of you.

To Bishop A.G. Reid Sr., You taught me how to be a better father because you weren't always there, but I love you RIP.

To Griselda Small, Thanks for allowing me to date your daughter and being a great mother In-law. I miss you RIP

To Shanita Peppers, for being a good friend and providing a place for me to get licensed. Love you Sis.

To Ivan Zoot, thank you for opening doors for me and showing real barber love.

To Bo Langley, You really wanted me to make it and I appreciate all you did. Miss you man, RIP.

To Lance Wahl. Thank you

To Michael Muhammad, for being there from the beginning of ABMAAM and holding it down for me on and off stage. Thanks buddy.

To Patrick Fox, you took what I shared with you and ran with it. We're not finished though.

To Dr. Aloysius Anaebonam, thanks for Bump Terminator.

To Beverly Pitts and E Hosea Hicks, for welcoming me to the PBS. Thanks

To Garland "Gwhiz" Fox, for showing me what was possible

To Nate Tony, Erica "Eklass" Kennedy, Adrian Hudson, John Feimster, Jay Kutti, Miquel Jessup, April Malone, Timothy Batten, Sir Reginald Wells, Christian Boe, Timothy Smith, Victoria Stokes, and Terah Da Barber. Thank you for your support.

To Mr. Kevin Mcleod, Mrs. Catherine Gammage and the entire Silver Oak Academy family, thank you for the opportunity.

᷅

Acknowledgments

Special thanks to Julius Thompson of Swaggedoutshot Photgraphy for his outstanding photography services.
To my online fans and followers: You made me write this book.

Contents

Foreword

The barber business is frequently referred to as the world's second oldest profession. The story goes that two cavemen went out on a hunt. They weren't successful which they attributed to their inability to see properly due to their hair hanging over their eyes. Legend has it that one caveman picked up a sharpened piece of flint and scraped some hair off the other. He handed the flint to his "client " and the other caveman did the same for him. They inspected their reflections in the river and decided that one of them looked better than the other. The other one was the world's first barber.

Ivan "ClipperGuy" Zoot

Not much has changed since, but everything is different in the barber business… And that is the way the barber business goes. Our craft is steeped in tradition, the way things have always been, and yet, we are constantly looking ahead to the next style or trend and the next technology we can embrace.

Al Reid has rightfully earned the title of "Most watched barber on You-Tube" and it is just one measure of his dedication and commitment to sharing the new and the old in the barber business. This book is Al's attempt to capture 30 years of experience and education for the purpose of enabling young barbers to learn from his experiences and veteran barbers to know that they are not alone.

His stories range from reliving his first haircuts to his passion for the latest and best our industry has to offer. Read this book once, then, read it again. Come back to it as a refresher and reminder of things you know, things you forgot and things you missed the last time you read it.

I am honored to know Al, call him a friend and contribute to this treasure trove of information.

Ivan Zoot AKA ClipperGuy

Introduction

Intro

Honestly, I didn't set out to be a barber. I installed and refinished wood floors, sold everything, from vacuum cleaners to education. I owned a body and bath store, and even pastored 2 churches. I did all of that before I slipped in through the side door as a barber. Now in my 50's, I guess you can say I've been a busy guy and even though barbering wasn't my first choice, it's been a constant in my life for

Alsmillions

over 25 years. This road hasn't been easy, but I learned to love and respect the craft and that made it easier. I've seen some good, I've seen some bad and a whole hand full of ugly. As with any other profession, barbering isn't a cake walk. The struggle is real my friend, because no hair professional is just going to move over and let you have some of their light to shine. You'll have to be willing to work hard and bring your own sun if you want to make your mark today. I shouldn't say "nobody", because there are a handful of barbers and stylists that will share their light. If you find one that will, hang on and cherish them.

I have seen upcoming barbers wandering like lost sheep, trying to find a place where the space is quickly getting smaller. I have also seen veteran barbers, frustrated and angry that barbering is blowing up and they have become too old to enjoy it. There was no fanfare, no accolades, no hair shows when they were coming up. Barbering was the job most people didn't want. You were considered a failure if you told your parents you wanted to cut hair, but today, times have changed. Barbers are signing autographs and negotiating product endorsement deals. I find myself somewhere in the middle of all of these and I'm far from hanging up the clippers, so I've decided to share most of what it takes to build a successful barber/stylist business. I think I know a little something, because I've built a thriving customer base 4 times in 3 different states, toured the country teaching thousands of barbers how to do it and I continue to teach hundreds of thousands on YouTube and other social media outlets.

I wrote this book to inspire, to inform, to teach and to ignite a new fire in my audience. A fire I hope will spread from one professional to another and throughout the entire hair industry making us all better. As a bonus, I have also shared what I call "wisdom cuts". Wisdom cuts are short wise sayings. I feel the Creator has blessed me over the years and I'll share them with you at the end of most of the chapters. Today, I continue to do what I feel I've been called to do and that's to help barbers and stylists become better. Stylists, forgive me if I happen to address barbers more in this book, but that's only because I'm a barber. I assure you that most of what I will share will apply to you as well.

Come with me, as I endeavor to share with you the wisdom and knowledge I know will help you find the missing pieces, or just reinforce what you already know and set you free.

Chapter 1 Anatomy Of A Barber

What is the anatomy of a barber? It's all that goes into making us what we are. It's the substratum, the rudiment of how a barber is built mentally. The creative ability to remove or rearrange hair so as to make men and women look and feel better. Barbers usually have an eye for detail  and the uncanny ability to scan a packed room and pick out the bad haircut in a matter of seconds. Barbers are visionaries, prophets of hair and we can see the finished product before we even get started. Barbers are bad! We can be judgmental, but not always in a bad way because many of us are just trying to learn. We know when the hairline is receding so we begin cutting the hair differently to camouflage the inevitable to keep our client looking good longer. That's what makes up a barber and these attributes are simply amazing. Barbers are entrepreneurs at heart, yearning for the day when they can open their own barbershop. They're the new modern day, white collar business men and women. We're CEO's and presidents with board members. Who would have thunk it?

With all of that being said, barbering probably wasn't our first choice when it was time for us to choose a career. Most will tell you that once they saw the art of barbering and saw how barbers had the ability to literally transform a man in the chair, that's when they were hooked. When what's inside of you connects with what the barber is doing for the client in the chair, that's when your life changes forever.

Do You Love Cutting Hair?

The fact that you've read this far tells me you have a strong affection and growing desire to cut and style hair. I can appreciate how you feel because after 26 years of barbering, I still dream and visualize the mechanics of cutting hair. I love what I do and I don't regret the long hours I've spent studying and practicing to be the very best barber I could be. Nor do I regret the money I've invested, and the blood I've shed trying to master shear cutting techniques. It's been a long road, but it's been all worth it and I can truly say that I'm proud to be a barber. I learned that true success starts from within and works outward. Your inward desire will cause you to acquire all the knowledge and training you can so as to enable you be the best at what you do. Yes, I still look forward to coming to work and attempting to cut that fade better this time for my clients. With every progression, with every new skill a barber masters, their love for barbering increases. These are the things that make a barber.

The Genesis

As far back as I can remember even before I gained a love for barbering, I always had a pair of cheap "house" clippers that I learned to use to freshen myself up between professional haircuts. Just like everyone else, I jacked myself up at first trying to cut my own hair, but I soon got the hang of it and I eventually started cutting my friends and neighbors for $5.00 each. At that time I never would have believed that I would be teaching across the country, making instructional videos and owning my own barbershop. After attending business school for computer operations, I secured a job at an insurance company as a data entry clerk. I entered new insurance policies in the system all day long and I was about to go crazy. Talk about boring. It was nothing for me to nod off with my fingers pressed on the keys and wake up to see a screen full of P's. I knew I had to get out of data entry fast. I was a natural salesman, I sold just about everything, including life insurance. I became a licensed life insurance agent, but never achieved salesman of the month. After a few years doing that, I went on to start my own wood floor refinishing business. I learned this craftsmanship on weekends and any free time I had with a good friend of mine, Robert Harley. He showed me how to be a wood floor master. The money was good, but after 10 years, the work was beginning to wear on my body.

I decided to go back to sales and landed a job as admissions director at a New York City business school where everything was great until the government uncovered fraud in many of the nation's business schools and changed the way business schools could be compensated for enrolling students. I was doing the same work for half the money I was previously earning. I was simply tired of getting into occupations that didn't have longevity.

It was during one of my weekly haircuts in a crowded barbershop that the notion came to me that the barbershop always had customers. It seemed like the barbers never went home and they always had large knots of money in their pockets. It also appeared to me that many of the barbers there didn't cut that much better than me. I would later find out that I really had no idea what it took to be a licensed barber. It was too late, I was already bitten by the bug, the barber bug. Suddenly, all I wanted to do was cut hair. I would stand outside barbershops and watch the barbers cut. I guess those barbers thought there was something wrong with me just standing there watching them as if I was a stalker. Nowadays, barbers can sit back in the comfort of their own home and watch all the barbering videos they want on YouTube, but we had none of that back in those days.

The Day I Jacked Up Carlos

In 1989, I enrolled at Apex barber school in New York City and that was the day I knew I discovered what I wanted to do. I was so excited I couldn't even sleep at nights thinking about my next day at school. The instructor told me he would let me start cutting as soon as I brought my tools. I remember him telling me how he thought I was going to do very well and he gave me an Andis master that he had in his words "just laying around." I was thrilled! All I

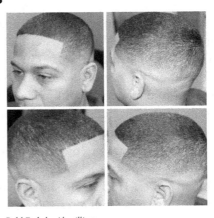

Bald Fade by Alsmillions

needed was a Andis T-Outliner and the Oster 76 with 3 or 4 detachable blades and I'd be set. I scraped up the $200.00 I needed and was ready to cut hair the next day.

I was ready and because I was there first I received the first walk-in. Haircuts are only $5.00 at most barber schools so people often take their chances just to save a few bucks. On this Tuesday morning, Carlos Herrera came in first. I'll tell you how I remember the day and his name later. Carlos was a tall guy and he was built like Hercules, so when he walked through the door, he had everyone's attention. Carlos had been there before, but the guy that used to cut his hair had graduated, and he was looking for a new barber. I was so nervous I could feel my leg jumping, but I didn't want to show that I wasn't ready. Carlos asked the instructor how good I was and the instructor said, "He's new but he's pretty good". No! Not when it comes to straight hair on a dude with a large head! I had never cut straight hair before and Carlos had plenty of it. Carlos was a six five Puerto Rican from the Bronx, who looked like he didn't play games. He said, "Popi, give me a bald fade, tight and not too high". All I could say was "No problem", but I was telling worse lies than the instructor. The only thing I remember about that cut was the initial baseline and then hearing Carlos say, "What the hell you doing Popi"? The blur cleared up and I was almost on top of his head trying to remove another line. I was making the line higher each time I tried to remove the previous line. It was hot, I was soaking wet and Carlos looked like he was wearing a yarmulke on top of his head. I turned Carlos into a Jewish man and he was hot as fire. I was two seconds from running out the door and then his girlfriend came in. I knew I was dead then. She said, "What the hell, not on your birthday" and Carlos said, "somebody better fix my head, now"! The instructor told me to go to the classroom in the back and wait for him there. I was out before he finished the sentence. I heard Carlos say "Where's that big head blank, blank, blank, going"? I was just glad to be out of there, but my relief was short lived. After only 10 minutes, the barber instructor called me back in, but I knew Carlos was still there. Why would he be calling me back in? Didn't he see Carlos wanted to choke me out? I came back in slowly, trying not to appear nervous and scared out of my wits. The barber instructor said, "Come on in Al, everything's cool, I explained to Carlos that today was your first day cutting and I fixed his hair to his liking". Carlos said, "No problem Popi. Sorry I went off, but today's my birthday and you know how it is. Tell you what, next time I come in I want you to cut my hair again. You're going to cut it until you get it right". All I could say was; "thank you" with a silly looking surprised look on my face. I made sure that every time Carlos came in, I cut his fade better and better. Before long, I had his fade clean and tight every visit. That incident and Carlos's promise helped build my confidence and I was able to get through barber school at the top of my class. By the way, guess who brought me a whole new set of tools at graduation? That's right, Carlos and he continued to come to me even after I landed my first licensed barber's position up in Harlem.

I shared all of that with you for two reasons; Most of us start out doing one thing and end up doing something else. I've had many jobs and a few businesses but barbering was what I really wanted to do. Secondly, every barber or stylist can tell you about their own messed-up-somebody hair story. I've heard quite a few over the years and they all have been pretty funny. Don't feel bad if you don't have one yet, just be patient, there's one coming.

Exodus

It wasn't until 2008 when I really made up my mind to take barbering serious. I went to the Bronner Bros. hair show in Atlanta, with only a few dollars. In fact, I only had fifty dollars in my pocket after I paid the admission for my wife and myself. It was obvious I didn't go there to buy the newest clippers or the latest barber gadgets. I was there to obtain information and knowledge. I had to find out what I needed to do in order to attain the next level as a barber and to be able to support my family with the income from barbering alone. I already had a small YouTube following from uploading hair cutting videos, so I wanted more information on how to take that to the next level. A barber named Alex Campbell is in my opinion the original trailblazer for the YouTube hair cutting tutorials we see today. He showed me what was possible and his work gave me the incentive to be better.

I went to every class I could go to that day and I soaked up what was taught like a dry sponge. I remember sitting in the class of a well known, talented barber, but he almost put the whole class to sleep. He's an excellent barber, but his teaching skills were dismal at most. A voice inside of me said, "You can do this". The voice was so loud and clear, I thought my wife said it, but I realized it wasn't her because she was nearly sound to sleep. I left that classroom on fire! I was excited, but I wanted to see more before I made a final decision. I remember walking by the Wahl booth and Garland "G Whiz" Fox was teaching a class on clipper cutting so I decided to have a seat. Mr. Fox was well informed, had a sense of humor and knew how to get his message across. I watched his every move until my wife came angry, tired and ready to leave. She was angry because I hadn't answered my phone and she had been searching for me for forty five minutes. She was fuming and even while Mr. Fox was teaching, he knew what was going on with us and addressed it. He said, "You better go man, she looks like she's about get all of us". We all laughed, but I was embarrassed that my wife had come to get me. We left, but I talked about the show the entire trip home. Mr. Fox had lit a fire in me that until this day has not gone out.

I came back to the shop the next day with a new purpose, a new desire to teach. I knew I could teach, because I had pastored for years, worked as a motivational speaker and product closer in corporate America. The only concern or fear I had was that maybe I was too old to make this new dream happen at almost fifty years old. I soon put that fear to rest and began preparing myself for the mission at hand. With the help of the Lord, I dug down deep and gathered all of my experience, and I asked Him for the wisdom and set out to make it happen.

In 2009, I founded ABMAAM, Average Barbers Making Above Average Money. ABMAAM was established to help barbers and stylists reach their full potential. While the focus is to help barbers put out better haircuts and master the art of barbering, we also understood how important it was to help barbers and stylists build their clientele quickly and to work more efficiently. Having this knowledge is vital to any hair professional aiming to be successful in today's society. Product knowledge, customer acquisition, and good customer service should be a major part of every hair practitioner's development. People are looking for those hair professionals who are the best practitioners of this knowledge. ABMAAM has been able to help literally thousands of barbers address the needs of their clients with this philosophy.

I went on to be the most viewed barber on YouTube with millions of views and hundreds of thousands of followers. In 2010, I traveled the country on my Emptychairitis tour teaching the ABMAAM way to build the barber's business. With the faithful support of the ABMAAM team and the many customers that purchased our products, we were able to fund the entire tour without any major sponsorship. I did however, receive major support and recommendations to teach at the Premiere hair shows around the country from Mr. Ivan "ClipperGuy" Zoot. At that time, Mr. Zoot was the director of education for Andis and was the closest thing I had to a mentor on my road to success. I will never forget the doors he opened and the support he gave me during my "come up" years.

Wisdom Cuts

You witness success happening to others, but do you truly believe it can happen to you? That's your biggest battle.

The ability to recognize and attach one's self to a positive flow is the key to going to the next level.

Success is knowing how to handle life when they aren't calling out your name anymore, buying your records, sitting in your barber or stylist chair. The decisions you make after you "succeed" are what's most important.

It's the simple things that make you great.

Chapter 2 So You Want To Cut Hair?

So you really believe cutting hair is what you want to do? Well, let me share some statistics that might be of some interest to you. The hair industry has grown leaps and bounds over the past ten years and sales of hair care products are through the roof. In June of 2014, Small Business Marketing research states that there are 440,000 bar-

Cutting my son Max

bers, 41,340 barbershops, 210,000 Beauty salons with combined revenue of 20 billion dollars. That doesn't include hair supplies and human hair sales.

New barbershops are popping up practically overnight and you can find one on almost every commercial block. This is also true in the urban areas where it's no big deal to see two or three barbershops and a couple of hair salons all on the same block.

Things have changed now though. I remember when you could just turn on the open sign and get ready for the customers to just pour into the shop. We could cut all day from walk-in customers alone, but those days are over. You have to hope and pray for a walk-in today. People no longer flock to your shop just because you open the doors. They have so many barbershops to choose from that just offering a haircut without the amenities might not be enough. There's everything from the national haircut franchises to the traditional barbershop trying to remain relevant in a time where most patrons know very little about the traditional haircut experience.

Do You Have It?

If you're a new barber or stylist coming into the business of hair, you must have what I call the full package; Good cutting or styling skills, creativity and excellent customer service. Excellent customer service will take you a long way, even if you're cutting, styling and creativity isn't that great. Remember; people love to be pampered and treated like VIPs'.

By now you should know if you have a natural ability to cut or you're like some who find it necessary to work harder to learn cutting styles and techniques. I do believe that some barbers are gifted with the ability to cut hair and they seem to have that natural hand/eye coordination already embedded in them. They have what I call the barber's eye. The barber's eye is the ability to see lines of demarcation, bulky areas and the finished haircut even before it's finished. Now of course, you can be taught to do all of the things mentioned, but it's definitely a whole lot easier if you can do it going in. It could sometimes take a person up to a couple of years to master observing and correcting lines of demarcations and cutting mistakes, so to have that gift is a blessing and a big time saver.

There's also something else that will tell you if you'll do well as a barber. Once an apprentice has been exposed to barbering, he or she will find themselves always thinking about cutting hair. They will dream about cutting, have an intense desire to watch haircuts being done and be ready to cut hair at the drop of a hat. This is why many apprentice barbers find themselves messing up their family members and whoever else will allow them to practice on their heads. If you're not going through any of this, then I would have to honestly question whether or not you are truly cut out to make it as a barber. One has to love to cut. You must love the process and above all, be ready to make the sacrifices necessary to succeed as a barber. Lastly, something you should also consider; barbers who do very well financially are not shy, withdrawn introverts, preoccupied with themselves. They're open, great to be around and able to interact with everyone. If this is you, then you might be on your way to a potentially rewarding career.

Get That License

No matter your skill level or how much you love barbering, everyone must be licensed to cut and style hair in their state of residency. There might be different requirements in every state, but having a barber or cosmetologist license is a must in every state. Check your local state barber board examiners for the laws and requirements for your state.

Some barbers pay to attend a barber or cosmetology school to acquire the hours needed to allow them sit for the barber's exam. Others might be blessed to find a master barber they can sit under as an apprentice to acquire the hours they need. The total hours needed may vary in every state so make sure you check your local state board for that information.

Acquiring your barber's license will require plenty of hard work and sacrifice. You will need to study everyday to perform well in class assignments and tests. If you're working as an apprentice, ensure you gather all the books and materials necessary to give you the information you'll need to pass your barber exams. You will need to pass a theory exam and a practical exam. If you should fail either one of these exams, you will need to prepare to take it again until you pass it. In most states, the post exam printout will tell you what you need to work on so you can put in extra study time in that area.

Whatever the case, do not stop until you secure your license to operate in your state. I've seen barbers get caught and fined for not being licensed and then have to pay hundreds of dollars in fines just to be eligible to apply for a license. Some hair cutters seem to feel that they don't need to be licensed because they cut well and follow basic sanitary procedures. That couldn't be further from the truth, because there's so much more you need to know as a licensed barber and the state needs to know who's operating where and if they are qualified to operate under state law. Don't play with this. Go to school or secure an apprenticeship, but don't work without securing a license.

Wisdom Cuts

Don't strive to look cool cutting hair, but strive to make hair cutting look cool. That will eventually open doors for you. If you seek to make the industry better, more doors and ideas will open up to you.

Don't let what other people do distract you from your mission. Congratulate, support, but stay focused on you. Your success comes with consistency and an understanding that your day is coming. Some of us get sidetracked when others have success and it throws us completely off. Don't allow the seeds of hatred take root, for this immature behavior. Keep your focus and stay the course.

Cutting hair without a license is like welfare, it's alright to get you on your feet, but you'll never truly get anywhere until you get off of it.

You're in a good place. Things are looking up and you now realize why you had to go through that dark and dreary mess. No more fear, no room for hate. It's all about reaching that goal and leaving negativity behind. The sky is crisp and clear. Enjoy it, and don't go back!

Whenever you are out of place, you will be replaced. Hold your position. You can't be everywhere and do everything. You probably think you're making progress, but truth be told, you're coming up short somewhere. Even the most successful multi-taskers' focus on one project at a time.

I got news for you; It's lonely at the bottom too, because no one wants to sit next to the guy at the bottom.

Don't expect someone else to see your dream and work harder than you do to make it happen. It's YOUR dream! Not theirs.

Your thoughts become words, your words become actions, your actions become habits, and your habits become your destiny.

Chapter 3 Customer Acquisition - Quick Start

Ask any barber what they think is the saddest sight in the barbershop and practically everyone will agree that it's a barber not cutting when everyone else is. Yeah, that has to be one of the worst feelings, right behind messing up a haircut and having to let someone else fix it for you. Sitting and waiting for a customer to come through the door is like dying a slow death. In fact, I call it "barber suicide". You're killing yourself and it doesn't make sense especially if this is how you plan to pay booth rent and take care of your personal responsibilities. You're going to have to work hard and smart for

Customer Acquisiton

your clientele or else you'll be cutting out of your house. There's no "maybe tomorrow" or "I'll do it next week" when it comes to this. You'll have to put on your big boy/big girl drawers and proceed to make it happen. Nobody is going to give you customers and it's not the responsibility of the owner/manager to get you clients to cut or style.

The first thing any barber or stylist must understand is that just sitting and waiting for the next walk-in to enter is not going to do it. Years ago, that may have been an option, but because of the number of barbershops and salons customers have to choose from, the heavy walk-in traffic we use to enjoy is now a thing of the past. A barber or stylist has to be proactive to make it happen today. They should always be promoting, sharing and getting the word out about who they are, what they do and where they can be found doing it. Laid back, reactive hair professionals don't do very well and suffer financially because of it. Whether you're a student just out of barber or cosmetology school or a veteran relocating to a new area, you'll both find yourselves in the same predicament. Unknown with no clientele and asking the question; "How do I build my customer base fast enough to help me take care of my responsibilities"?

Be Proactive

Pro-activity is the key. You cannot wait, hesitate, or procrastinate when it comes to building your customer base or you will be watching others cut and style each and every day. Some people are drawn to a shop based on service and quality and then there are others who are drawn to a shop based mainly on price alone with the hope they will receive a decent experience with good results. Whatever the case, a barber must know that he or she can no longer just sit and wait. The barber must be proactive, not reactive, especially if they want to secure a strong customer base. The proactive barber gets the referral after a cut, the proactive stylist never hesitates to make the next appointment before the client leaves the chair and the proactive hair professional never sits around chatting it up when they could be out handing out fliers, sending out new customer promotions, or posting their latest hair cut on social media platforms.

Successful barbers care about their clients. They treat them as if they were a family member and they take special care to give them the best service every-time. Good barbers are customer service oriented, outgoing and charismatic. Remember, everything you do for this customer, bad or good will be shared with someone else, because each customer is your walking and talking billboard. You want people stopping them and asking them who cut their hair, because it will reinforce to them that they're looking good. Your customer will readily brag about the services you offer and you'll receive new referral business on a weekly basis.

30/60 Plan

I like to do a 30 to 60 day customer acquisition campaign when building my customer base. I turn it into a game and I compete with myself, attempting to do better everyday. I use a combination of personal contacts, customer referrals and social media interactions to build over the next two months. I don't even factor in walk-in traffic, because I consider that gravy, the cherry on top of the sundae.

Let's start with personal contacts. I suggest that you physically talk to ten people a day about what you do, where you do it and how you can be found doing it. You can do five people in the morning and five in the after-noon. You can do more, but make sure you do at least 10 a day. That's fifty to sixty personal contacts a week that could potentially give you five to ten new customers a week. Take this exercise seriously, be very consistent in doing it and it will yield you a huge return. Be patient, you probably won't see anything the first week or so, but then slowly but surely people you've talked to will begin to drop in.

My goal is to acquire five key clients I can make my friends and lock in to my barbering services. For example, if they have a razor bump condition, I'll put them on my treatment regiment and once they see the bumps clearing up, they're locked in. They now believe in me and feel indebted to me for helping them. These clients may be well known in their community, very active in church, or members of a social club, or civic organization. As a result of the relationship I've built with them, I'll encourage them to share my contact information with everyone they know.

Here's a sample of what you could say to get potential customers to try you out.

Customer Invite

"Hi, my name is John and I'm a new barber to this area. I work at the XYZ shop down the street. I'm looking for a few clients who can appreciate a good haircut with excellent customer service. You probably already have a barber, but I would love the opportunity to share my barbering services with you. Here's my card with all of my contact information. Don't hesitate to give me a call when you're ready".

You can also offer them an introductory half off for their first visit as an incentive to try you out. This incentive really works and half is better than nothing when you're building your clientele. Be sure they understand that it's a onetime offer and only make this offer if you feel it will really get them to come in.

This is basically all you need to say. Make sure your card has your photo on it along with one or two pictures of your work. In chapter 6, Branding Yourself, I'll explain why it's important to have your picture on your business card or flier.

Keep plenty of business cards and fliers and leave them everywhere you go, especially where you do business. Most restaurants, supermarkets, retail stores and offices have places where you can leave your business card or flier.

*Business Cards - Yes the old standby, but with a new twist. Business cards with your picture on them in a creative way, to grab the attention of the viewer. Just remember to keep it in good taste and keep it simple. www.gotprint.net [http://www.gotprint.net] has excellent prices on business cards and fliers. You can design them yourself or have them do it for you. They do all kinds of promotional printing.

*Fliers - Fliers still work. If you're willing to give them out, you'll have good success. You can purchase 5000 4x6 fliers for a little over $120.00.

This is a small investment when you consider how much business you can draw if you distribute them correctly. Do not put them on cars and doors because more of them will be thrown away than will be read. Nothing beats giving a flier to a potential customer, introducing yourself, sharing a quick story and inviting them to come see you. This is the best way to hand out fliers.

Now let's look at customer referrals, the best method in my opinion to build your client base quickly with quality clientele. Word of mouth is still the fastest way to get the word out about anything now that the internet and social media has come on the scene. Imagine a small army of your clients, sporting your haircuts, going out each day showing them off and telling people about the services you offer. Now put some business cards and or fliers in their hands and you now have your own marketing team out there reaching people you could never reach alone. Your clients go to work, social events, clubs, churches, lodges and other places where there are large gatherings of people. Most clients would be more than happy to help you build your business.

*Here's a sample of what you could say to get your clients to help you out.

"I want to thank you Matt, for your patronage. There are so many other places you could go for your haircut... Thanks for trusting me. By the way

Matt, you know I'm new in this area (or just getting started) and I really would appreciate you sharing my flier (or business card) with anyone you know who would appreciate a good haircut and quality service". That's basically all you'll need to say to get them to help you out.

*Websites / Social websites - Next to television, the internet is the fastest and economical way to reach most people nowadays. I prefer social websites (YouTube, Facebook and Twitter) to personal business websites because some social websites allow you to target the people in your target areas. Just request their friendship and once they approve your request, you can let them know what you do. You can send out pictures of your work, weekly updates, specials and discounts to get the attention of prospective customers.

The days of turning on the open sign and having the customers rush in are over for the most part. There are so many barbershops competing for the same customers and a customer today not only has a backup barber, but a backup barbershop. With this in mind, barbers must utilize all of the available methods and resources to attract good clientele to patronize their business.

Smart barbers are proactive! Always moving, always doing something and constantly searching for new ways to build their client base. They're on top of the latest haircutting and styling trends. They attend hair shows and workshops to re-energize and educate themselves to deliver the services they've learned to deliver better service to their clients.

The Difference Between A Client And A Customer

There's a big difference between a customer and a client and if you're going to be successful as a barber or stylist you should know the difference. Clients are usually found in service oriented businesses where trained, skilled practitioners such as doctors, lawyers and hair care professionals provide the services needed. The client usually has an ongoing, trusted relationship with the business, will make repeated visits and establish a long-term relationship that could last for many years. They would also seek advice and require ongoing assistance for whatever circumstance or need they might have. In contrast, The customer, is more focused on the product to be purchased and has no allegiance to any one store. A customer can go to Walmart in the morning and to Target in the afternoon or to McDonalds today and Burger King tomorrow. There's really no allegiance to anyone, store or product, especially if the product is on sale or discounted somewhere else. In fact, customers are short term and undependable, but clients are long term, dependable and loyal. When a customer needs a product or service, they might get it from the closest, cheapest place they can find but a client will travel distances, make appointments just to get the product or service from you. I teach and believe that hair professionals who convert customers to their clients should always go one step further and make the client their friend. A friend will always patronize and support you, follow you if you move and refer their family and friends to increase your client base. Cultivate relationships so that you become indispensable for what you know and who you are. If you can get people to need and depend on what you do and how you do it, you will never experience the problem of lack of clientele.

Yourself

Before you can really get serious about building your clientele, you must first know and be clear on how much you want to make a week. You should have a goal set and you should be competing with yourself to reach that goal. Notice I said; "competing with yourself". That's right, your competition is not with the guy in the next booth or even the shop down the street. Your competition is with yourself. That old lazy, "I'll do it tomorrow self". This "self" is the very reason most people are not further along when it comes to growing their businesses today. They've lost too many battles with themselves to go to the next level.

The "G" A Week Breakdown

So let's say you want to make $1,000.00 per week. The first thing you must do is to find out how many customers you'll need to offer your services to in order to get there. If you charge, say $20.00 per cut, you'll need to cut the hairs of at least 50 customers/clients to make $1,000.00 that week. If you leave it like this, it might not seem realizable, but if you break it down, you could be on your way to making a $1,000.00 in no time.

*The Break Down

  50 x $20.00 = $1,000.00

50 customers a week on a 6 day week is roughly 8.5 customers a day.

50 customers a week on a 5 day week is little over 10 customers a day.

Now, you can clearly see how many customers you'll need to make $1,000.00 per week.

*How Will I Get The Customers?

1. Talk to at least 10 people a day about your business. Go to the malls and busy areas to "press the flesh" and to tell people who you are and what you do.

2. Hand out at least 20-30 business cards and or fliers a day. Give a bunch to trusted clients and let them give them out at businesses, clubs, churches, etc.

3. Work your social media. Post your latest hair style pictures, give out helpful advice to establish a following, post specials and post regularly.

4. Work the "Refer 2, Get A Free Cut" method. Tell your client for every 2 customers they refer, you'll give them a free or discounted haircut.

More Ways To Build Clientele

1. How to acquire new customers

You can be the best barber on earth, but if you don't have anyone to cut, you're just a broke barber. The barbers that work the most do these 3 things; Promote, Promote, Promote. That's right, you must always be in the "Promote Mode". Always promoting yourself, promoting your business, promoting your skills. People will learn who you are and what you do with your promotion, so you want to "always be promoting". Here are some ways to promote:

*Referral Incentives - Give your existing clients a reason to tell someone about you by giving them a ½ off or free haircut when they bring in a new client. Whenever you have down time, you should take at least 1 hour and go to the malls, parks or to places where people gather to eat or to be entertained. Give out your fliers and business cards to everyone you can so they will know who you are, know what you do and know where they can find you. Public relations is your lifeline, so always make time to do it. Let your work be your best form of advertisement. Whenever you do a cut with designs that you feel will draw a lot of attention, give the client a few of your business cards to give out when they're asked about the cut. Bargain promotions, get people's attention and that's what you want. Cut the kids hair for $5.00 per head or free for 3 hours just to get them to come in and see your work. Once they come in, the rest is up to you.

*Walk-ins - Be ready! Be ready when they come in. Greet them with a smile and be sure you and your station look the part. Regardless of how you get the walk-in, you must put your best foot forward. Do your consultation and make sure you understand what the customer wants. Find ways to lock the customer in by asking about their concerns and identifying problems. (I.e. receding hairline, razor bump problem, dry scalp, etc.) Once you help address any of these concerns, you can bank on this customer becoming a client.

Wisdom Cuts

When in business, make sure you're offering the people what they want or you will have a limited market. Often times, we offer people what we like and we end up with a storage room full of products.

Does Wendy's show a commercial one time and pull it? Does Ford let you see its new pickup commercial twice and think that's enough? No! Absolutely not! So why do we think when we give out a flier in the community one time or have one promotional event for our shop, we've done enough? You have to keep yourself in front of the people. Stop wasting money on stuff that don't matter and advertise you!

Your business building decisions should be made with the mindset to increase your clientele, not to show off what you have. People aren't trying to make you rich, so you should downplay your benefits and play up what they will get by doing business with you.

Why are you looking for oranges to grow when you've planted apple seeds? You can only harvest what you plant.

When promoting yourself, your task should be to get people to see or hear about you at least twice from different sources. This will confirm to them that patronizing your business is a good idea.

Social media is the best thing to happen to entrepreneurs ever, but most entrepreneurs don't know it.

You're always dressed to the max, but you're always sitting and waiting for a customer to come in. Invest more money in promoting your business and be a busy, well dressed professional.

Unless you're a sports commentator, wasting your time arguing about Mayweather and the Lakers is not going to change your financial situation. Use those words and aggression to promote you and win over some hair cutting prospects.

Things sometimes look bad and they may be bad, but you need to look for the good in the bad. So you only rendered 10 hair-cuts to people today, but that's 4 more than you cut last week at this time. Things are getting better!

You may not be making enough to get out of debt, but you made something! Keep pressing, sacrifice more, get out of your comfort zone and above all.... Don't give up!

There are two things you should always remember if you want to win over people for whatever you have in mind:
1. You can't clean a fish until you catch it and
2. You have to know what the fish wants to eat.
Stop trying to sell folk, change folk, save folk, awaken folk, transform folk, convert folk when you don't even have what they want to get them to listen. The best bait you can offer.... Is yourself, doing it, not talking about it.

Chapter 4 Customer Retention

Client retention is just as important as client acquisition. What's the use in working hard to obtain clients and customers if you're not going to provide good customer service to keep them? Some customers are always looking for better deals and service, so if you don't do certain things to keep  them, you might just lose them. We've talked about the difference between a customer and a client in the customer acquisition chapter and we know that some customers are fickle; they change frequently, so if you plan to hold on to some of these guys you'll have to stay on top of your game. Notice I didn't call them clients. Clients are happy with you for the most part and unless something major happens, they aren't going anywhere. Here are a few ways to keep your clientele in place and have them remain loyal to you for years to come.

The best way to keep a client is to make the client your friend. Friends are loyal, friends are dedicated to each other and friends will let you cut their hair just because of the friendship. Could you imagine your friend coming into the shop and sitting in someone else's chair? Of course not. By making the client your friend, you solidify the business relationship. Does this mean you have to go out for drinks or watch the game with your clients? No! Absolutely not. You just need to do what is reasonable for a person who appreciates the client. For instance, you might remember special events that are important to them, like birthdays, graduations, social events, etc. Or you could simply treat them like you would treat a casual friend without necessarily hanging out with them. The key is to make the customer your client and your client your friend.

Friendships aren't built overnight, don't expect the both of you to be singing Kumbayah after only two weeks, so be patient. The more often you see your client, the more the client will open up. You should begin to look for shared interests. Maybe you guys like the same football or basketball teams, belong to the same fraternity, or have children in the same school. Whatever it is, this will allow you to have something in common. You probably won't have this commonality with all of your customers, but it's always a plus if you do.

My client friends are the best. They appreciate what I do for them and how I make sure their hair looks its very best. I've helped many of my clients get rid of their razor bump or dry scalp conditions. I look after them like they were a family member and to show their appreciation, they tip very well, bring refreshments on days they know I'm working hard and they have no problem telling anyone that has hair on their head where they should be going. I call this "locking a client in". Once you lock in a client with friend-ship, benefits and services, they aren't going anywhere. The problem most barbers have with clients hopping chairs and shops comes from the fact that they never took the time to lock the client into them. A client can get a good haircut at many shops, but they won't find too many barbers addressing their needs like I'm suggesting you do.

It's Not About You

I've worked with many barbers over the years and there were some that believed they were God's gift to mankind when it came to hair cutting. There's nothing wrong with being confident and believing that you're good. The problem comes when you act like customers should be grateful you took the time to cut their hair. I know there are customers and clients that are almost impossible to deal with, but this is the profession you chose. You'll have to remember you're in the people business, suck it up and treat your clients' right. I've witnessed barbers being rude and abusive to clients, berating them for being late or not conforming to their way of doing business. There's nothing wrong with encouraging a client to follow your business procedures, but you can't berate them like little children if they fail to do what you ask them to do. Kindness and professionalism have always been the call of the day. In fact it's very simple to remember what to do. Just treat your clients like you would want to be treated and you will never have a problem. Remember! Don't trip on yourself! Stay humble, so people can like you or you'll be an empty chair, no customer having, sad can't pay your rent, two bit broke barber. When every barber shop closes except yours and you're the only barber left with a pair of clippers, that's the day when you can treat your clients like you're doing them a favor. Until then… They're doing you a favor.

8 Ways To Retain Your Clients

1. Give your clients a free haircut on their birthdays when they've been with you for at least 6 months.
2. Give discounts to clients with large families. If a client gets his hair cut and brings his boys', give him a few dollars off to show your appreciation to him for bringing them all to you. This will serve as an incentive to let you give all his boys haircuts. I started doing this when I noticed my clients were letting other barbers in the shop cut their boys' hair while I cut my clients hair. No disrespect to anyone else, but that's my money going into someone else's pocket.
3. Offer on-line booking for your clients so they can see your schedule and book you whenever they want. You can send out mass notifications and special discount offers. Once your customer expresses their satisfaction with your work, you'll want to get them in the system so they can book you for their next appointment and you'll have all of their contact information. Now you can call or write them if you move or just want to notify them if you plan to be out of town.
4. Give candy to kids when they come. This will help them sit still and make you their best friend. Also, if you can do parts or simple designs, give the boy one on the house with the parents' permission of course. The child will forever want to sit in your chair and will have a fit if his parent tries to

take him to another barber. You would have created a faithful customer for years to come.

5. Offer a punch card and give your client ½ off or a free haircut after 10 punches. Use a business card and punch it with a hole puncher. Be sure to get a hole puncher with different shapes from a craft store. They have designs like a heart, a square, etc. You don't want somebody punching a card themselves with their own circle punch. This will give your customer another reason to come to or wait for you only.

6. Be attentive to your client. Show that you care about them. Offer remedies for razor bumps, dry scalp or dandruff and perform the treatment for free. Make sure the treatment is safe and proven. On slow days, offer free hair shampoo with their haircut.

7. Be there when they show up. The fastest way to lose a client is to never be there when they come to get a cut. When they walk in, greet or acknowledge them like you're really glad to see them (Because you are). Let them know how long their wait should be and make sure they're comfortable. This goes a long way with a client because every customer wants to feel important and appreciated.

8. Be sure to have a VIP version of your basic haircut posted so the client can choose to receive those services. VIP services may include hot towel and facial cleansing service, nose and ear hair removal, eyebrow cleanup, shampoo/hot oil treatment and a head or neck massage. Offer the services you feel comfortable doing and make them available as birthday and gift packages.

10 Reasons Why You Should Be Using An On-Line Booking Service

1. It allows you to easily acquire and organize new and existing customers. Book a future appointment as soon as they leave the chair. Know how many clients you have at all times.

2. It helps you remember your clients' name, birthdays, how they look and hairstyle so you can easily prepare for their next appointment.

You can take pictures of the clients hairstyle for future references. Send out specials and discount notices to all of your clients.

3. It helps you look professional and more organized and your clients will be impressed by your system of booking and addressing their needs.

4. It allows you to send out mass notifications and holiday well wishes. Let all of your customers know in a few minutes when you will be on vacation or away from the shop or salon.

This avoids having clients coming to the shop unaware that you're out of town. Helps prevent clients going to another practitioner.

5. Get an additional web promotion from having your business listed on Google through the online service.

6. Avoids pricing and service confusion. Both you and the customer knows the pricing and services to be rendered.

7. It allows you and the client to book weeks and months in advance with notifications to help you remember.

8. Avoid double booking. Remove the frustration of having 2 clients arrive for the same appointment. Clients hate being double booked and you could lose them.

9. Contact all of your clientele easily if you decide to move to another shop or salon.

10. Make more money when you implement this on-line booking tool.

The Renegade Customer

I've thought long and hard about this type of customer for years now. Every barber or stylist with 10 or more clients can bear witness to this type of customer. The "rebellious, can't wait, won't call, come in at the busiest time of the day" type of customer.

A renegade customer is one who rejects barber shop protocol and conventional behavior. A renegade will never really get along with the program no matter how much sense it makes. They want and need to do things their way, which is usually the complete opposite of what you're trying to do. Now don't get me wrong, I'm all for thinking out of the box and being different to the extent that it doesn't hurt you or disrupts others, but I also believe in order. First come, first served and if you're in a rush and can't wait, make an appointment!

Renegade customers usually go undetected for quite a while or until your clientele picks up. You see, when you only have five customers, the renegade customer is always a sight for sore eyes. You're glad to see them because whenever they show up, that's a few more dollars in your pocket. As a matter of fact, renegade customers love it best when you're never busy, so they can come in whenever they want. They can just pop up at 10:00 A.M. or 7:00 P.M. and you'll be sitting there, in the chair, waiting for them or anyone to appear for that matter. They love to see the look of joy on your face when they walk in, but that look will start to change as your clientele grows and you get busier. It won't change because you don't appreciate their patronage or dislike having them as a client. It will change because all of a sudden, they start to show up when you're busy cutting someone's hair. Now when they come in, you have one customer in the chair and two customers waiting and suddenly it's not how it used to be. That look of joy is now a look of frustration, because since you've started to get busy, you have asked your customers to call to minimize their wait time. Oh, I forgot to mention to you another secret about renegade customers... They don't like to wait. They hate it! That was one of the main reasons they started coming to you in the first place; you never had anyone in the chair and so now you have a dilemma. How do you continue to show that you appreciate the business of your first real client, when the client won't call and continues to come in at the most inopportune times and expects immediate service? How do you deal with that?

Well, here's how I dealt with it and let me tell you now, it rarely works with renegade customers, because they want you to change for them. First, I would excuse myself one moment from the client in the chair and take them to the side, calmly and quietly tell them how long the wait would be. After they express to me that they couldn't wait, I would tell them how I appreciated their business, but to avoid them having to wait in the future, it would be good if they called and made an appointment. After saying this, I don't care how nice you say it, their eyebrows will rise as if to say, "Oh, you big time now"? They will then tell you how busy they are and they wouldn't be able to keep an appointment, they lost your number, etc.

I'll give them my card again and I'll even offer to let another barber with a similar cutting style to mine to cut their hair, but I cannot and will not push them in front of a waiting customer. By the way, that's what they expect and want you to do. If you do that, you will lose the other waiting customer and they will continue to come whenever they feel like it and expect immediate service.

Now remember, that's what I do the first time it happens. Renegades will be renegades, so the very next time, they will do the same thing. This time, I only acknowledge them, but I continue cutting the client in the chair. After a few minutes they will come over to me and ask how many I have and then I'll tell them, not mentioning our previous conversation unless I want to start an argument. I'm still nice and friendly, but they now understand this is really about business and if they don't respect my time, then they'll have to wait or let someone else cut it.

At this point, I'm prepared to lose them as a customer. Do I want to lose them? Of course not, but I can't jeopardize the relationships with other clients to please a renegade customer.

They will resent you and talk about how you've changed. They'll say how they remember when they were your only customer, but you can't let that bother you. Renegade customers are necessary. All barbers and stylists need them to get started. Once they help us get started, they move on to a new upcoming hair professional. The saga continues....

Chapter 5 Cutting Techniques & VIP Services

Here are some tips for achieving a better looking cut that will set your haircuts apart from the rest. Your client will also enjoy the attention to detail and the relaxing application of hot towels which will allow them to experience something few barbers will ever do.

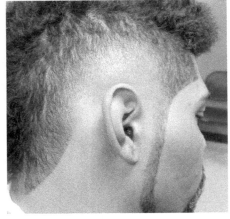

Burst Fade by Alsmillions

1. To make your low cuts and line ups look cleaner and sharper, it is important that you lay the hair down with the clippers. Don't just comb the hair in place, cut it in place. Constantly comb wild hairs in place to be cut during the lineup. To cut hair in place, you must cut downward on your Caesars and faded areas, giving you a smooth blend.

2. Use a blow dryer when performing a hair cutting service. You can use it while combing out the hair to loosen it for cutting. The hair will stand up better with heat and make it easier for you to cut evenly.

3. On low cuts and skin fades, before you line up the cut, apply a hot, wet towel to remove loose hair, dirt, grease and debris from the head. This

allows the hair to lay down for easier line up. There are two reasons why you should adapt this technique. Firstly, it allows you to get a cleaner looking cut and secondly, it just feels good to the client. For curly or wild hair that won't stay in place during the lineup, use spritz or a holding spray to freeze those hairs in place. A light mist, followed by a little heat from the blow dryer will do. Once the hair is dry, line it up as you would normally do for a clean, crisp lineup.

Grooming & VIP Extras

Take care to remove hair from ears, nose and neck. Also trim wild hairs from and around the eyebrows remembering to obtain clients' permission first. If your client's face is visibly oily and dirty, it is a good idea to wipe it down with a warm towel or an alcohol pad before you clipper shave them. This will do two things: Keep you from infecting the client with his own dirt and debris and give you a cleaner, easier clipper shave. Lastly, be sure to completely wipe away the debris and not just spray an astringent over loose hair, skin and debris, creating a mud pack when wet. This process will help your clients avoid or get rid of razor bumps and set you apart as a barber.

There are many things you can do to give your client a better cut, but if you really want to get paid, you must remember that your client loves to be pampered. We sometimes think only women love pampering, but truth be told... Men like it too. Barber swagger is about how you make the customer feel. So here are a few things you can do to pamper your client and increase your income.

Self Training Techniques

When learning precision cutting and design work, you learn faster when you're around others who practice or master those techniques. Barbers who work alone or isolate themselves from new techniques, etc., tend to learn it at a slower pace or even forget most of what they've learned. So if you work alone, remember to stay plugged into cutting videos that show-case your interest. Watch at least 2 cutting videos a day and practice, prac-tice, practice.

Your confidence will come by doing and watching those whom you per-ceive to be skilled. Keep your mouth shut about your weaknesses and your strengths. As you get better, remember how you used to cut and know there's still more to learn. Practice until the process of cutting becomes automatic.

Cutting Through

Cutting through is a mind over matter technique I developed to help me get through rough haircuts at the end of a long day. You know about those days if you've been cutting for a minute. If you don't, let me describe it to you; it's a Saturday and you arrived early and you've been cutting practically all day. Your arms are tired, your feet are tired and all you want to

Cuts by Alsmillions

do is lay back and rest. You're finishing up a client in the chair and your appointments are done for the day. Just about the time you prepare to remove the cape from the client's neck and let him go, another client walks in the door. Oh no! That's what you say, because you were ready to jump in the car and go home. If it was anybody else, you would just tell them you're done for the day, but this is a special client. This is a good paying regular, who has a last minute engagement and didn't have time to call you or book an appointment online. That's what they all say, but it is what it is. You agree to cut his hair and you turn away like a little boy whose mother has told him he can't go out to play. Keep in mind, this client may have a beard or a specialty cut like a burst fade Mohawk and it will require some work. It's a 50 minute haircut when you're feeling fresh, so how do you prepare yourself to give this client the same quality cut he gets when you're fresh and not tired?

First of all, ask the client for 5 or 10 minutes to make an important call or use the restroom. Use this time to refocus and think about the task at hand. Drink a beverage (non alcoholic), walk around a bit, stretch legs, back, fingers, and get ready for the work to be done. You see, you're preparing yourself this way so you can give your client your best. You want his beard to be symmetrical and sharp, the fade needs to be blended well and the lineup must be precise. You'll need to dig down deep and tap into the part of the brain that perks you up when you get good news or causes you to be your best when very important people are watching. See, your body operates the way it was designed to, but it can be pushed to the next level if the mind is strong enough. For example, you're on your way home and you feel the need to relieve yourself. There's no reason to panic at this point because it's just a light notification and you're just 15 minutes away from home. By the time you're 5 minutes from home, it seems like you're about to explode. Why is that? Your brain sends messages to your bowels and your bladder that you're almost there and they react to that message. When you finally arrive home, you're running to the bathroom to relieve yourself. Your mind caused all of this to happen quicker. If you had been home already, you could have waited a much longer time before heading to the bathroom. That being said, if you can control how you see or process a situation, you'll have better success.

Now that you know what needs to happen, this haircut should be easier. Focus on the detailed areas first. Lightly outline the beard, get rid of all unnecessary hair, and keep the client brushed off and clean. Step away for a minute if you get tired, use your mirrors, and take your time, don't rush. Let some good music play, start a good conversation, let them talk and systematically complete the haircut.

Cutting Procedures: Afro, Caesar & Shaved Head

The Afro

The Afro haircut is one of the most difficult cuts to master, but once you get the hang of it, it's pretty easy to do When cutting an Afro, your objective should be to make the cut round from the top of the left ear to the top of the right ear and slightly oval around the bottom of the ear, across the neck and to the other ear. It should also be symmetrical on both sides.

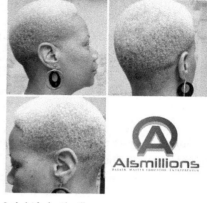

Ladys' Afro by Alsmillons

Pick hair out to the fullest extent using a blow dryer on hot. Keep the dryer constantly moving to prevent burning the hair or the clients skin. Once hair is completely picked out and standing up, use your clippers to cut the most obvious uneven section. Don't try to get a perfect cut at this point. You are only trying to set the framework for your Afro haircut. Once you've done that, pick it out again and now begin to neatly cut the shape you want in. Stand back off of the cut every few minutes to make sure your cut is shaping up evenly. If the hair is really soft and moves easily, use a spritz to freeze it in place.

Using Spritz - Spray the hair with a spritz until you can see it resting on top of the hair. Pick the hair out again to distribute the spritz throughout the hair. Apply heat again while picking hair out and let hair stiffen up. You can now cut the hair without it moving or laying down.

Once you have the shape you want with all of the wild hairs cut off evenly, you can begin lining the cut up. Once the lineup is complete, finish the cut with your shears.

The Caesar

Caesar haircuts are fairly simple to perform, but one must have the basic procedures mastered to ensure a nice, clean cut every time.

There are 2 types of Caesars; Light and Dark. A light Caesar is usually a 1A or a #1 with or against the grain. Note: Whenever you go against the grain with a particular blade, it cuts more hair than it would if you were to cut it with the grain. (Ex. A #2 would look like a #1. 5 if you cut the hair against the grain).

If your client has waves, he or she might suggest that you go with the grain to avoid losing the bulk that makes the waves look full and thick. If that's not their concern and they want them cut lighter you can most likely go against the grain.

For this example, we will cut the hair with the grain. Take your 1.5 and begin cutting the hair with the grain following your comb. You should comb the hair first with the clipper following the comb to place the hair in the direct path to be cut evenly. Follow a consistent pattern from left to right or right to left until you have covered the entire head. Once you've done that, you will probably see wild hairs sticking up all over the entire head. Grab a 1A and then repeat the same procedure as before, taking care to remove and or lay down standing hair. Remove all remaining wild hairs with your shears. Now dust the client off and line them up.

The Shaved Head

When shaving your clients' head, it is very important that you do it correctly, especially if you expect them to come back. I have outlined a few simple steps to help you leave your client completely pain free.

1. It can be difficult to shave a head that has too much hair on it, so it may be helpful to cut the hair prior to shaving. Use the lowest position on your clippers and cut the entire head evenly. Be careful not to press too hard so you don't scratch or irritate the scalp. Dampen the scalp with a hot towel for about 1 minute prior to shaving.

2. Apply shaving oil, gel, or cream to the entire area to be shaved. Massage into the scalp thoroughly as this will help prevent razor cuts and irritation by providing a protective layer between the skin and the razor. There are now new shaving gels on the market that break down the hair and make it easier to remove it with the razor.

3. Going slowly and with the grain is essential for a smooth, painless shave. Try not to re-shave the same areas more than two times to prevent skin irritation.

4. Apply a good astringent, aftershave or an anti-bump lotion to help soothe and protect the newly-shaved head.

Barber Swagger And Do You Have It?

Lately we've heard the word "swagger" used to describe rappers, movie stars and athletes. We would hear; "That so-and-so brings a whole new swagger to the game". What do they mean by that? Here's what the urban dictionary says it is:

Photo Shoot 2015

1. How one presents him or herself to the world.
2. How a person handles a situation.
3. A person's walk, A person's style.
4. To conduct yourself in a way that would automatically earn respect and command attention.
5. Your perfume or cologne, your jewelry, your trendy clothes, sunglasses, etc.

The above may describe a person with swagger and you might have some or all of those qualities, but still not have "Barber Swagger"

You see, barber swagger is not about the barber, it's about what the barber brings to the customer. Remember, barbering is about the customer. What can you do for the customer? True, if you already have swagger, it's easier to share it, but if you don't, You better get some.

So then, barber swagger is:

1. How the barber presents the client to the community or world. - Whether it's the brother in the hood or the lawyer in the courtroom, can you give them a swagger cut? A cut that will turn heads and make them look well groomed.
2. No matter what happens to the client in the chair, the barber handles it quickly and professionally. From accidentally cutting the client to fixing a bad haircut they received from another barber.
3. You give the customer a walk of confidence and style
4. Their excellent haircut and neatly shaved face commands respect and attention.

5. When they leave your chair, they feel like putting on their best perfume or cologne, their best jewelry and trendy clothes. All because they feel better and you, my friend have given them a new look, a new confidence, a new attitude, a new SWAGGER! Only barbers with swagger willing to use it to make the customer satisfied and happy can claim true Barber Swagger!

Sometime ago, I cut a gentleman who happened to be blind and of course I gave him my best. Just when I got ready to remove his cape. He told me this:

"My brother, I felt the care in your hands and the freshness of the soap you used when you washed your hands. The aroma from the oil you used really made me feel at ease when you shaved me. You seem to be a big guy with a big heart, some people don't appreciate that though. I feel that you've touched every hair on my head and my senses tell me that I look good". A compliment doesn't get any better than that and every client should feel that way when you're done.

Why you should understand Pseudofolliculitis Barbae

Pseudofolliculitis barbae is a skin condition caused by improper shaving and bacteria, which is commonly known as "razor bumps." First the hair is cut too short which causes the hair to grow inward beneath the skin. This is also known as an ingrown hair. This hair continues to grow beneath the skin and causes irritation and swelling. The swelling smothers the hair follicle and combines with bacteria producing pus. This is the first sign of infection and the infected area will also itch and get only worse when the area is scratched and or rubbed.

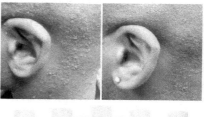

Pseudofolliculitis Barbae (Razor Bumps)

Over 60% of people with curly hair suffer from this condition. African American and men of color with curly hair lead all ethnicities when it comes to this condition. Most barbers have seen this condition on their customers and just don't know how to treat it. If a barber takes the time to learn how best treat this condition, they would have a client base that would be off the charts.

Pseudofolliculitis barbae can be prevented by shaving the hair with the grain, using a good quality astringent or razor bump formula. It is of the utmost importance that one avoid close shaving for this will cause the hair to be cut below the skin level and lead to bumping.

Wisdom Cuts

Think of your clippers, trimmers and shears as an extension of your arms and they will do what you need them to do.

When learning to cut hair, you should expect to do better every time. Remember what gave you trouble this time. Rehearse in your mind what you did or what was done to correct it.

Some people are like a poorly cut Afro: It looks good until you pick it out.

Chapter 6 Be Brand New - Branding Yourself

I remember watching old western movies and cattlemen would brand their cattle with their symbol or mark to make their cattle identifiable so cattle thieves wouldn't be able to steal the cattle and pass the cattle off as theirs. Branding has been used as an identifying tool to show possession for thousands of years. Today, we use branding to promote companies, products and personalities. By using themes, logos and the attributes of a personality, advertisers and publicists can send a message to help people remember the product or personality. For instance, a publicist might have their client donate

Alsmillions for Bump Terminator

their time and money to a great cause to establish the person as a caring individual. They could also create a product for the client designed to help people in need. All of these and the way the client communicates his or her message will become their brand, so whenever you think about people in need, you would also think about this personality.

Your goal when branding yourself is to have your name and face synonymous with the product or service you represent. For example, Coke is synonymous with cola, Listerine is synonymous with mouth wash, Chapstick is synonymous with lip balm, Kleenex is synonymous with tissue and we could go on. All of these companies have done an excellent job at causing you to use the brand name as a generic term. Case and point, Cola is the generic name, but Coke, Pepsi and RC is the brand name. If you can get people to use your brand name when speaking or thinking about a product or service you've done a successful branding job.

What do you want people to think about when they see you are hear your name? That's the question you should be asking yourself as you start your career in the hair industry. Do people remember you when they think about getting their hair done or see a fresh haircut or hairstyle? Your name and face should be synonymous with what you do. That's the main reason I suggest you include your photo on your business cards and fliers. This will help them visualize you when they think about needing your services. This is the first step towards branding yourself with your customers, friends and industry associates.

How To Brand Yourself

When branding, it is important that you brand yourself both as an expert and as an interesting individual. Why an expert? No one wants to be advised by a novice or someone just going through the learning process, so showing yourself to be knowledgeable about the subject at hand is particularly important. Why interesting? Just being an expert at something can sometimes be boring and unappealing. One needs to be memorable; you should stick out in the minds of potential clients. Whenever they need your services, you are the first person they think of. Some of you might think you have a problem already. You might be saying, "There's simply nothing memorable about me". Don't be silly. Everyone has something memorable about themselves; they just need to know what to look for.

You'll be surprised to know that the simplest of things could qualify you as an industry expert, but it will require hard work and a great deal of consistency.

Consistently Consistent

Your brand will have to be seen and understood if you want people to associate the product or message with you. You'll need to be consistently consistent about advertising and promoting your brand. Whatever form of advertising one chooses, it needs to be repeatedly broadcast so that people see it continuously. The more they see your logo, hear your message and see your product, the faster they will associate you with that product or service. Everything you do (with a reason) is an event. Smart branders know how to make an event out of buying a new pair of clippers. These mini events allow you to associate yourself with another product and at the same time give you legitimacy in the barbering community. This sound like it would be easy to do, but in fact, it is one of the most difficult things to do. People just seem to fail when it comes to performing a task repetitively. You would think the lack of money is the reason, but today, most social media advertising is relatively free and all one needs to do is post their message consistently. When students ask me how many times they should post, I know they're not going to be consistently posting because they're counting already. You'll need to post as long as it takes to catch on, so there's no real number that I could honestly give you. It's about how effective you want your advertising campaigns to be. Ford doesn't run their truck commercials five times and quit. No, they run those commercials hundreds of times a day in as many markets they can in order to get their message across about their trucks. In the 70's and 80's, Coca Cola had us singing their jingles to help brand its name and boy did it work. Coca Cola has made its brand synonymous with cola. When you think cola, you think Coca Cola.

The Expert

Being good at something doesn't help you if nobody knows about it. And that is where branding comes into play. Let's walk through the process together. Who are you, and what are you good at? What gifts, skills, or knowledge sets you apart from the competition? The answers to those questions point us to the essence of your personal brand. Whether you're a master barber or beauty consultant, your brand should position you as an expert in your field, and it should reflect the specialized skills or knowledge that your competition doesn't have, or doesn't communicate. A few years ago, I noticed that many of my customers, including myself suffered from Pseudofolliculitis barbae or razor bumps. Pseudofolliculitis barbae is the inflammation of the hair follicle caused by bacteria and irritation. I learned everything I could about this condition. I searched medical books and spoke with dermatologists to understand how and why so many African American men struggle with this condition more than anyone else. I learned that the coarse and curly hair that many of us have had a tendency to curl inward. If cut too short, this inward growth would bring dirt and grease with it and would cause the skin to get irritated. On top of all of that add scratching and or rubbing continuously until bumping occurs. I literally became an expert on the causes of folliculitis. So much so, I began looking for serums and treatments that would work to rid my customers and myself of this condition. I later partnered with Bree Technologies and became the national spokesman for Bump Terminator razor bump treatment. People trusted and respected my advice because the information I shared with them on video would turn out to be true for them. I never passed myself off as a dermatologist. I would just share what worked for me. People began to follow me on YouTube because they appreciated the information I was sharing and they trusted what I had to say. I built my brand on honesty and one of the best when it came to barber training. Barbers knew that I would give it to them straight so If I said a product was good, barbers believed me and went on to buy it.

Don't Be Shy

Next, so people will remember you, forget about your business qualifications for a moment; Think about your personality for a minute. Are you shy, withdrawn and to yourself? Well, if you are, that will need to change. People are not attracted to shy, withdrawn individuals when they're looking to follow, support or receive instruction from a person. Confidence in branding is the key and shy or withdrawn people don't come across as being confident. You must be charismatic and have the ability to lead if necessary. People want to be on the winning team so you must show that you have the ability to win. Your conversation must be positive, progressive and fearless and you will attract a following of people that believe you have your act together. Now understand something, an egotistical, self centered, show off, will also find it hard to draw a good following because people will dislike and refuse to support their efforts. Be wise, be humble and you'll do well.

At The End Of The Day

What makes you unique? Are you outgoing? Charismatic? Do you have a sense of humor? What are you passionate about? Do you truly care about others? Do you have any additional hidden talents? As I told you, I built my brand on honesty and trust so you should identify two or three personality traits that make you unique, and you've identified the "personal" part of your personal brand.

This is the part that makes you human, likable and palatable. If people don't like you, they won't listen to you, follow you and definitely won't patronize you. So to sum it all up, you must advertise your brand consistently, have something of substance to offer that you truly believe in, don't be shy or withdrawn. Show care to people. That's all it really takes. Get to work!

Social technologies, such as blogs, Facebook and Twitter have allowed entrepreneurs to build warm markets and relationships. This allows them to become known, connect directly with their audience and build relationships on a global scale. As an entrepreneur, you need to become the brand.

1. Become an expert on something that relates to your business.

2. Establish a website or a blog under your full name.

3. Learn how to be a good source by positioning yourself as an expert in that field or market.

4. Generate brand awareness through networking.

You should be connected with other entrepreneurs in your industry using social networks and commenting on blogs. Networking is one of the best ways to become known in your industry. By creating relationships with people in your audience, you can grow your business and your brand long-term.

The four rules of networking that you should keep in mind are mutualism, giving, targeting and reconnecting.

*Mutualism: You have to create win-win relationships in business, making sure that you don't benefit more than the other party.

*Giving: Help someone out, before asking for anything in return. This makes people want to support you.

*Targeting: You want to be very specific to the types of people you network with, in order to save time and to attract the right people to your brand.

*Reconnecting: Never lose touch, that way, networking contacts remember you when new opportunities surface.

Wisdom Cuts

If you do not reinvent or refresh yourself, your brand will get stale and people will look for something new.

Be brand new!

Chapter 7 What Are You Worth?

You're a consummate professional. You've worked hard to get where you are and you've paid your dues to be the best barber/stylist you can be. You use quality products, clean towels and implements. You don't cut corners when it comes to the customer. You advertise whenever you can, your workplace is clean and inviting and you treat all of your clients with honesty and respect, so why are you afraid to charge

Cuttin' Like A Boss!

Cuttin' Like A Boss Promo 2012

them what you're worth? How much do you think your services are worth to the client? It's worth every penny and probably more. Cheapskates might not want to admit it, but they wouldn't want an unlicensed, unskilled barber cutting their hair with dirty clippers and wiping their face with soiled towels. Quality requires money, it's not free, so don't cut yourself short. If you don't charge the money required for you to give professional services, you won't be able to give them. People who don't want to pay your asking price may need to move on. For every customer that moves on, there's a customer who appreciates your price and service. Stay in business, get what you're worth.

What's The Problem?

The economy is gradually regaining its ground and almost every industry has suffered a loss of business on some level. The hair industry is a little different because while there's been an increase in products and services exchanged, the price per customer has not increased. It has in fact, slightly decreased. Barbershops, especially in the inner city and in poorer neighborhoods still charge as little as eight or nine dollars for a haircut. The same shops were charging seven or eight dollars more twenty years ago for the same haircuts. How could this be? Why are men haircuts so cheap? Well, that's easy; So many new barbers in the business competing for the same customers and each barber or barber shop undercut the other in the hopes to win the customer over. The customer now believes that anything over $15.00 is too much to pay. We've done it to ourselves, so what's the real solution?

Since you have to compete anyway, why compete over a ten or twelve dollar cut? You would do better if you worked a little harder for a higher paying, quality conscientious customer willing to pay more. I know I've suggested in the past that you should lower your prices to stay open, but some of these barbers are getting ridiculous. Someone needs to put a stop to the nonsense. When I realized that the same guys that make it rain in the strip clubs and spend big money to buy big bottles of liquor are the same ones asking for a discount in the shop, I knew this definitely had to STOP!! I said to myself, "I make him look good so he can go throw money away"? Well, let me get mine before he does. Now how do you stop something that is basically out of control? How do you now command a higher price and get it? Hopefully, I can share some tips to get you what you want.

Don't Feel Bad Because You Charge More

This is the first mistake barbers make. They feel bad that they charge more than the rest. You should only feel bad when you're not giving the best service you can give for the money requested. You should be proud of your skills and the services you offer and constantly seek to be the best at what you do. Remember, you don't have to be a "master" or "Guru" in this industry to command the kind of money you want. You just need to love it enough that you do a great job every time. If you've worked hard to horn your skills and you're providing the best service possible, you have no choice but to charge accordingly. There's no need to boast or brag, just state the facts, and let your clients do the bragging. Always remember this; anything you want people to think about you shouldn't come from your lips. Let it come from your clients and customers. Let them hear it, read it but never let them hear it coming from your lips. You don't want to be caught bragging about how great you are, because it devalues and cheapens your brand. It can also be viewed as a turn off because tacky, insecure people brag about themselves, so try not to do it.

How To Add Value To Your Business

Barbers make their second mistake when they believe they can just raise prices and the customer is just going to agree to pay more. You'll need to do more than that. You have to add value to your existing services. The idea behind added value is that, the customer gains a perceived benefit without having to pay for it or pay very little, compared with its value to the customer. For example; A pair of sneakers for $30.00 and a pair of sneakers for $200.00. The reason a person will pay $200.00 for a pair of sneakers when he or she can get some for $30.00 is the perceived added value. Whether it's the name or athlete associated with that sneaker, the consumer believes $200.00 is worth the expense. Do people really want a good deal, or do they want a good value? I believe they want both and if you're wise, you'll learn to combine the two to differentiate yourself from the pack. Adding value is a way to raise your prices and stand ahead the rest. I always teach students to offer abbreviated services that give the client a taste of that VIP experience without cheapening the service. People need to experience what they're asked to pay more for, so if you're looking to raise your prices, start by offering a complimentary service to allow the client to experience what you do. Once a person experiences value, it now makes sense to pay more. You will be surprised to see clients expect to pay you more, because what you offer is worth every dime. Ideally, you want to offer something that has a low cost to you, but a high value to your customers. You should only feel bad when you're not giving the best service you can give for the money requested. You should be proud of your skills and the services you offer and constantly seek to be the best at what you do. Remember, you don't have to be a "master" or "Guru" in this industry to command the kind of money you want. You just need to love it enough that you do a great job every time. Don't boast and brag, but just give them the facts. Let your clients do the talking and I'll say it again; "Anything I want you to think about me can't come from my lips". Here are a few more ways to add worth and value to your barber shop or salon:

*Offer A Strong Guarantee - This helps you gain customer confidence and will reduce buyer's remorse. The guarantee should be meaningful and not too restrictive. Offering to refund money or to redo a service if they are not satisfied. This is an easy way to reduce pre-sale apprehension.

*Free Bonuses - Anything from an extra product to a free service like a hair and scalp treatment to help show the value of your services. People love free things, especially when they are not expecting them.

*Do Things Differently - Creating a unique model or approach to doing business sets you apart from your competition. If you approach business differently, or have a different method or process that works better than your competitors, use that to your advantage. Even if it seems small, sell the benefits of it. Show them how you are different. Take care of your clients in a unique way. Look at everything you do and do it better. Constantly push yourself to do better.

*Be Upfront About It - Clearly communicate who you are and how your shop or salon is different. Having a clear marketing message not only helps weed out those that don't want to pay for your services, but it also adds value. Customers know exactly what you do and how you can help them. You are saving them time and they appreciate that.

*Be An Industry Expert - Isolate the largest problem your clients have with their head or face. Then deliver the service and put an emphasis on solving that concern. Offer products that they can only get from you. That works to help lock in your client.

*Quality Assurance - Industry standards and accreditation can be valuable. This added value shows you care enough to take the time to reach an industry-accepted level of excellence. So any hair show awards and advancements, be sure to post them so everyone can see.

*Look Upscale - This includes every part of your barbering business, from location, signage, furniture, decor, etc. Set the ambiance and tone of the shop through dress code, music and smell. Your bathrooms and lounges should be spotless. Use sign in sheets and customer data forms to make sure you can best address your client's needs. If you can afford a receptionist and or a hair wash assistant, this will upgrade your shop, help free you up and allow you more time to focus on the customer. Remember, if the client sees it, it has to be perfect and seamlessly match your shop's brand.

*Know The Client - Keep detailed records on the client's likes and dislikes. This includes everything from hair color to favorite sports teams. Some clients prefer phone calls, others email or text messages. Make sure you keep the notes in the same place. If there's ever a transition with you or your shop, the client should not have to go through a major get-up-to-speed curve with the new personnel. I cannot tell you how many new clients I've gotten simply because the previous barber dropped the ball during a transition.

*Be Proactive - Get referrals and don't be afraid to ask your client to spread the word about you. This is also a great way (maybe the best way) to drum up new sales. Long term, being proactive will increase both customer loyalty and word of mouth.

*Pamper The Client - Make the client feel important by doing little things like including a hand-written Christmas card, give-away sports, or theater tickets. Even more importantly, make the client feel trendy/cutting-edge and encourage their belief that they made a good decision making you their barber.

Wisdom Cuts

You can get a $1.00 hamburger or a $10.00 hamburger. There are customers for both. You just need to know which one you're prepared to sell.

Practice walking in the position you want to be in. Once you get in that position, carve out a niche for yourself to increase your value.

When people don't respect your talent or gift, they won't give to you what they would gladly give to someone else. Whether you're a barber standing behind the chair or a speaker on a stage, be sure to get what you're worth.

One must know his or her own weaknesses. Above all, you should not put yourself in situations where you cannot be of any help to yourself.

A barber should not look like a bum! His or her job is to make others look good. We must start with ourselves. You don't have to break yourself buying new clothes and jewelry. Just buy quality clothing, keep it neat and clean. Keep yourself well groomed. Self worth starts with how you look and feel.

What you used to do, and the job you used to have and how you used to look, means very little today. Move on!

Chapter 8 New On The Scene

There is no right or wrong way when it comes to getting along with people, but the best way to handle existing barbers when you're new to the shop is to just be cordial. Be friendly without trying to be friends, if that makes sense. You're not there to share your life story and talk about your personal business, nor are you there to make a friend for life. You're friendly enough for them to tell your client you'll be right back, but not friendly enough for them to expect you to go out for drinks after work. No, it's not about being anti-social; it's about

keeping some distance between the two of you to avoid over familiarity. When people grow too familiar, they think they can ask you personal questions, remove products out of your drawers and cabinets and in some cases, be very disrespectful. People tend to keep their distance when they don't know you to avoid causing a problem. Joking around and snapping on each other is bad business and barbers should refrain from this behavior, because it never ends well. I've seen barbers start in the morning and by the end of the day, they were packing their belongings and moving on because somebody said the wrong thing. When a barber goes to work, the goal is to make money and that can't happen if they're caught up in unproductive behavior. A successful barber or stylist understands the importance of getting along with everyone and this means that everyone stays respectful and remembers why they come to work in the first place. Be there to build up your clientele and make money. So many barbers and stylists seem to forget why they're there and get caught up with interactions that don't produce dollars and cents. You can be friendly and not need to get chummy with the barber next to you before you've had a chance to get your first hair cut. Remember, most people have a problem sharing potential customers with anyone, so they're not really trying to be your friend. They just want to know how good you are and if you're going to be a problem for them in the future. I suggest that you keep it business friendly. Friendly enough for them to take a message or tell your client when you'll be back.

What You Shouldn't Expect

As a barber new to the scene, there are a few things you should not expect to happen. You are a licensed professional, an independent contractor and you are in business for yourself. The owner or manager of the barbershop or salon is not responsible for building your clientele. You'll have to do your on advertising and customer acquisition. See chapter 3 on how to acquire customers. Don't expect anyone to give you anything. You'll need to get out there and make it happen, because sitting around waiting for a customer in the barbershop can be frustrating and not something you want to do every day. Your rent will be due every week and don't expect anyone to feel sorry for you and give you a break, especially if you've been just sitting around waiting for a customer to walk in. That's a guaranteed slow death and I don't care how good you cut hair. You need customers to pay your booth rent and maintain your lifestyle, so you'll need to be real serious about what you need and how you're going to go about getting it. Now, some of you may work on the clock and get paid by the hour, which makes you an employee. In this case, the owner or manager would be responsible for advertising and bringing in new business. You'll see this arrangement usually at the national haircut franchises, but don't expect to make big money right away no matter which compensation plan you're on. It's going to require that you focus building that clientele quickly.

8 Things A New Barber Should Do

8 Things A New Barber Should Do

1. You must have the ability to listen and give the client what they want. Too many barbers ignore what the client wants and gives the client what they want the client to have. Even if it looks good to you and the whole world, unless the client asks you to do what you think is best, you should be doing only what the client wants.

2. You're Clean! Your sanitary procedures are on point. There should be no place for cross contamination or potential infection to your clients. Your hands, your implements and other items are sanitized or sterilized according to your States barbering specification. Start out fresh by showering daily and applying nice cologne of your choosing. Apply lightly around the wrist and arm area, so when you're working around your client, they only get a hint of the fragrance. Keep your nails well manicured to avoid scratching your client and or catching excessive dirt and germs under them. Nobody wants an unclean or a smelly person working all over their face and head, so be mindful of this and your clients will certainly appreciate it.

3. You're in the house! You must be there when the client arrives. Be on time for every appointment. There are many good barbers who constantly miss haircuts because they aren't there. I made 20% of my clientele from barbers who constantly stood their clients up.

4. Can you do it? You must be able to do the service correctly, professionally and in a timely fashion. Speed is also important. You can't keep a client in the chair all day and expect to make above average money. Get them in and get them out.

5. A Good Personality - Must be cordial with a sense of humor, not nosey, but a good listener. A good barber must be able to keep information to him

or herself, must not be combative, not offensive, honest and able to get along with anyone.

6. A good barber must have the ability to make people comfortable, to bond with them and to find some common ground with the client. Example; Sports, fraternities, and so forth.

7. A good barber must be self confident and have a strong passion for the barbering profession. If you love it, you will do it well. Become a student of the game. Go to hair shows, study books, watch videos and other barbers to learn all you can. Sit next to barbers you perceive to be better than yourself (Iron sharpens iron).

8. Finally, a good barber should be licensed. Do it the right way, ladies and gentlemen and you'll spare yourself a lot of time and money. Going to school gives you the fundamentals and knowledge you'll need to work safely and proficiently. Holding a license can also permit you to acquire advantage of career opportunities exclusively available to licensed practitioners.

Who's In Your Circle?

That's the question you should be asking yourself as you grow your business. Your peace of mind and maybe your success will depend on you knowing who's in your circle. You may not have thought about this before, but you need to be aware of the friends and associates you have. You want to be honest with yourself here and call a spade a spade so to speak. You don't want to say certain people are your friend if they haven't proven themselves to be your friend. Put them in the right category and save yourself the problems. Some of us don't really know what a friend is. Having lunch with a person and talking about making money, doesn't mean he's your friend. She may like all the things you like and the two of you may often go out on the town together, but that doesn't mean she's your friend. Until you've really spent some time with her and she's demonstrated that she's got your back, she's nothing more than an associate. Friends are trustworthy and honest with you. They don't look to take advantage of you because their friendship is unconditional with no strings attached. We make the mistake of calling almost everyone our friend and that's how we get into trouble. Think back for a moment, all of the times your business got out or your name came up in some drama, it was a so called friend who put it out there. Most betrayals are done by people we call our friends so we all need to be very careful of the type of people we include in our circle and call our friends.

The best way to build a good friendship is to give it time. Give the association at least a year, so you can see the type of person you're hanging around with. Test them. Tell them little things you don't really mind other people knowing just to see if they'll tell someone else. Watch them, to see if they have character. Do they always talk about other people? Especially those you would consider close to them. Chances are if they'll tell you personal stuff about their sister, your information doesn't have a chance with them. Watch how they are with money. When you guys go out to eat, do they offer to pay or are they always waiting for you to grab the check? Money is big so you should really take your time vetting them on this one. The next time you're with them alone, drop 5 or 10 dollars to see what they'll do. If they pick it up and give it back to you, you might have a keeper, but if they put it in their pocket and don't say a word, you'll know what you're working with. I've had to learn the hard way that the joker I was running with was no good and really couldn't stand my guts, but that was my fault for rushing in so quickly and not taking my time. I also ignored the disrespectful manner they handled their other friends and associates. What made me think they wouldn't do the same to me? That was an ego flaw on my part. Evidently, I felt that I was such a great person, they wouldn't dare do that to me. I know better now and you should too.

I have listed a few more people we may have in our circle and might not recognize:

*The Disinterested Party - Won't help you, but they won't try to hurt you either. They respect what you're doing, but they're really into what they're doing to get close you.

*The Faker - Will openly support you, but privately wait and pray for your demise.

*The Opportunist - Will support you as long as they can shine and benefit. If that doesn't happen, you won't see them.

*The Leech - Comes off like a friend, but is always looking for a meal or something free. They never want to pay for anything, but will always be around.

Wisdom Cuts

Identify the Judas in your life. Keep an eye on them or get rid of them because he will betray you when he or she gets a chance.
Build your success on your own name, and then you'll have something of substance to say when people meet you.

If you run a business out of your extra bedroom, garage or warehouse, your customer just wants the product you promised. Don't get hung up on trying to impress the customer on how big you are or what you're about to do... Impress them with your product and customer service.

In all you do, seek to maintain your moral compass. I don't care how misguided your compass needle might be, you know how you want others to treat you. If you can look at yourself in the mirror and honestly say you're doing the right thing, then that's what you'll have to live with.

When you're a giver, you'll always have an audience. When you're a taker, you'll soon run out of people to take from.

Chapter 9 It's Just Business

You Don't Know Everything

As an educator, I found that the most difficult barbers to reach and teach are the one's making good money already. Barbers assume their techniques and procedures are on point because they have a decent clientele, but that's not always the case. We've all seen clients sit for hours, leave with a bad haircut, walk out the door and

then return for more in two weeks. Like barbers, some clients don't know what they don't know. In other words, they don't even know their haircut is not up to par and lacking a professional look. Most of these clients never had a hot towel shave or a facial service done, so they really don't know what they're missing. Once a client is exposed to professional barbering services, they'll never settle for less again. A good barber will remain open to knowledge and seek to be up on the latest techniques and procedures to better address his or her client's needs. Barber and stylists should get advanced training at least once a year to stay up on the new products and services available in the industry. The day the barber understands that he or she doesn't know everything, that's the day they'll give themselves a raise. Advanced training is an essential and vital part of growing your barbering business. Every time I learned a new technique or procedure, it increased my income. Get all you can.

Not A Hustle!

I know you've heard it, or you probably said it when explaining how hard you were working and you used the word "hustle". The word hustle has been used in the streets to describe someone working hard and making a lot of money. The person is called a hustler and he or she is usually involved in some illegal activities. Hustlers don't care about the person they are getting their money from, neither do they care how they get the money. If they need to lie or cheat, that's what will happen because a hustler is only concerned about getting the money. Barbers and Stylists shouldn't operate that way. Good hair professionals care about the client. They want the client to be happy and satisfied with the service given so that they will return and tell others. Hustlers no longer care to see the people they take advantage of.

I have however, seen barbers treat clients like tricks in the street. Talking and treating the client in an unprofessional manner, not caring about the look of the haircut or style and or over charging the client for the services offered. There's no place in the industry for that type of behavior and I wouldn't call that individual a barber. True barbers have a different mindset, and definitely not the mindset of just a guy cutting hair. No, we don't need any hustlers, barbers thinking like hustlers or barbers thinking they're hustling.

Money Coming

Every barber should be on top of his or her money. Your money is the life-line of your business, so you should know how it flows. A barber should always be aware of the pay weeks, holidays, tax season and above all, the slow days and weeks, so they will know how to best manage their money. For instance; if you know a holiday is going to fall on a Thursday, you should also know that Friday and Saturday will be slow days. Most people get their hair cut before the holiday, so chances are you won't have your regulars to cut on those days. You will however see new walk-in business on those days, because people who are always working take those days to look for a haircut. It's a good idea to offer specials on post holiday week-ends to activate your dormant customer base and get them to come in.

Good client management is very important. Try to keep your clients on a schedule. I know some of you like having all your people come in at the same time, so you look busy, but that could be a two-edged sword. You shouldn't want your people hanging around for hours waiting to get a cut. It's just not good barber management. Your people get restless and begin to eye other barbers. They see that you don't seem to have a grasp of good time management and it will eventually work against you. The only way to control your business is to control your business. When you have 5 or 6 clients watching you and wanting you to hurry up, it's not a good thing. Put your ego aside and manage your clientele or else you won't have anyone to manage. Put your people on a schedule and stick to that schedule and you won't have the back up. At the end of the day, you'll have less confusion, no walk outs and you'll make more money.

Good Barber Etiquette

The fastest way to lose a client is to offend a client. Having an understanding of good barber etiquette will go a long way to helping you gain and keep your clients. Here are some of the mistakes barbers make every day.

A. Ignoring the client. Give your client your undivided attention. Don't carry on long conversations with others and completely ignore the person sitting in your chair. They may not say anything, but they probably won't come back after a few episodes of that. Your client should feel like they are the most important person in the shop when they're in your chair.

B. Avoid talking good or bad about another customer in front of your client. This shows disrespect to the client not there and it makes the client present wonder what you say about them when they're not there. Just don't do it.

C. Watch your language and subject matter. You never know who's in your chair and you don't want to lose a good client because you want to "keep it real". Don't be silly. You're also disrespecting your fellow barbers and their customers. You could get into some real trouble if you cause another barber to lose his client. Everyone doesn't want to hear about your latest sexual escapades or how many "F" bombs you can drop in a sentence. Clean it up!

D. Maintain excellent hygiene. I shouldn't have to address this, but you'd be surprised how many barbers and stylists fail when it comes to maintaining the proper hygiene. Barbers smelling like weed and hot sauce is not what a customer wants to smell when receiving a service. Take a bath or shower every day and use deodorant. Brush your teeth and carry mints or gum for fresh breath throughout the day. If you eat a hot dog and onions, your customer should never notice. Don't lose a customer because of bad hygiene.

E. Not prepared. A barber that is never prepared is simply on borrowed time. It amazes me how many barbers come to work without supplies and the essentials to perform their work professionally. Don't be the "Can I borrow your stuff"? barber. Get your own supplies and be prepared for whatever might happen that day. Your client and your co-workers will respect you for it.

F. If you make a mistake, let the client know. Don't cut a plug out of your clients head and not tell them. Let them know what you did and then do all you can to fix it. Even if you must acquire help from someone else. Your client may not come back, but at least, you were honest and some clients will stay with you just because you were straight with them. Do the right thing, it always pays off in the end.

G. Respect your fellow barber and treat them like you want to be treated. Whether they're standing next to you in the shop or typing on a keyboard thousands of miles away on the internet. We can't lose focus from our goals. We must be wise! Don't let jealousy and petty beefs cause you to miss your money and end up in jail or worse. It's just not that serious.

The secret to making good money as a barber in today's economy is to do the things that most barber won't do. I just outlined for you the things many barbers struggle with when it comes to customer service and how to run your business. If you'll do them… You'll get paid! You'll work every day and you'll have more customers than you'll know what to do with.

Wisdom Cuts

When doing business, be careful dealing with those that are not really the decision makers. Also, just listen! If you listen long enough, you will find out what you need to know.

In business, you don't need to know everything, you just need to know how to surround yourself with those that do.

Never think you're the only one making it happen. You only read and like what you like and post. Big mistake! One must always know what one's peers are doing on some level. Self absorbed people are always asking what happened.

Because you maintain a heavy online presence and people see you in pictures posing all across America, that alone won't necessarily translate into dollars and cents. Your product must answer a need and or your work must cause people to appreciate you. This in turn will create a motivated buyer who's more likely to buy from you.

The grass is greener on the other side because you don't take care of your grass.

When you want to do something, you'll find a way, but when you don't want to do it, you'll find an excuse.

Don't deal with people who can't keep their word because they'll make you a liar.

Chapter 10 Why You Need A Mentor

Earlier on, I shared with you how I was reluctant to devote all of my time working as a barber. The fact is; I just didn't believe that barbering could provide all the income I needed to provide for my household. I always felt that I had to have additional sources of income because the money I made as a barber after expenses was never enough. Someone stated that there's no

My first meeting with mentor Ivan Zoot 2009

deficiency of knowledge out there, just a shortage of people asking for it. I don't quite know why I never searched for a mentor coming up, perhaps I didn't even know how to get one. I guess I imagined once you received your license to cut, that was all you needed. Sometimes, when you're young, your ego gets in the way and you don't even know what you don't know. A barber friend of mine had an uncle who was a barber and his uncle gave him some clippers and imparted a few nuggets about cutting hair to him. I just thought I was on my own, so I figured I had to make it happen myself. As I mentioned earlier, Mr. Ivan "ClipperGuy" Zoot opened doors for me and my ABMAAM organization to teach at some major hair shows around the country. That was definitely a blessing in disguise!

Today, you can go on-line and get all the advice you want. You can watch how to cut hair tutorials, learn about new products and services and even get some sound advice on how to build your business. You had to go to hair shows to get any advanced education or training. To be honest with you, I never heard barbers talking about going to hair shows or anything like that. You picked up what you could from the older barbers who would share what they knew. Many barbers wouldn't share their secrets due to fear that the student would then become their competition, so most of the time, they only shared the basics.

I know you believe you don't need a mentor. You're probably saying, "I got this! Nobody needs to mentor me", but that couldn't be farther from the truth. As an apprentice, a novice, you don't even know what you don't know yet. Back then, I didn't even know what to ask, let alone give an answer to do it. I was just feeling my way around and hoping I was doing right. It's still that way with everything that's new to you, so you want to be open to learn and that brings me to the most important question:

Are you approachable and teachable? I ask because if you aren't, you might as well skip this chapter now and move on to the next one. Mentors can't work with individuals who are not teachable. I didn't say slow, because you can be slow and still be teachable. I can't tell you how many barbers I've had contact me and claimed they wanted me to mentor them and the minute I began sharing with them what I knew, they began sharing with me what they thought they knew. Every time I said something, they tried to one up what I just said or they would talk over me while I was talking. They knew everything already. I couldn't tell them anything, so why were they there? They were there for a hook up. They just wanted me to "put them on" so to speak. They wanted me to put their video on my YouTube channel or do a video showcasing their haircuts, but they didn't really want me to mentor them. I can hear those barbers saying, "Isn't that what a mentor suppose to do"? Well, yes, that's one of the benefits of having a mentor, but that's not the main benefit. The student would need to demonstrate that they're learning the skills and applications taught them. They would also need to show good character and conduct themselves in a manner where the mentor would be proud of them.

Choosing A Mentor

Mentors are usually well known in their field of expertise and their good name and professional brand is at stake, so anyone that leaves with their recommendation must represent them in a positive light. Why would a mentor give a barber access to his circle of friends, business associates and industry contacts if the barber hasn't proven him or herself worthy of that? Despite what you might think, good mentors choose you. Even if you ask them to mentor you, they will and should take the time to see what kind of person you are. To see if there's a potential for good growth and a successful outcome.

Every barber seeking a mentor should ensure their motives are right. You never want to give people the impression that you're just using them. Once that happens, your mentorship could be over, that's not the way you want to begin your career. You never know who you'll need again, so as much as possible, try to be respectful and professional towards others.

The Benefits Of Having A Mentor

David Upshur

Some barbers don't understand the benefits of having a good mentor in their life. To have someone who has already paved the way down the road you're trying to travel is huge. Most barbers never get this and struggle their whole career, because they had no one. Wouldn't it be great to have someone advise you on the best tools to invest in, someone to encourage you and give you that moral support? Imagine having someone financially stable who could possibly invest in you and your dreams. I wish I was mentored. I spent so many years second guessing myself, afraid to move forward, scared to try, because I had no one to help and no one who even cared.

Today I understand that a good barber mentor could warn you about the industry pitfalls and save you years of pain and frustration. It took me almost 20 years to identify my niche and feel confident about my income opportunities as a barber/educator. A mentor would have shown me my options a whole lot sooner. He would have motivated and encouraged me to take different paths. Then again, maybe that was the path I needed to take. We all need inspiration, but most people are so busy, into themselves or just don't care about what you're doing to inspire you. Even if you could inspire yourself from within, it's never the same as hearing an inspiring word from someone else. The very thought that someone who's successful at doing what you're trying to do cares enough to invest their time, energy and maybe money to help you reach your goal is huge! The mentor wants you to succeed and if he or she is good, they will be the cheerleader when you need one or the stern voice of reason when you need that also.

Your mentor should have something going already, so helping you by letting you walk through their doors is a good thing. It's the ultimate blessing to be able to have a master barber as a mentor who also owns his or her own shop. Good mentors can and should be an access door to success. You're getting on the job training from someone you look up to and wants you to do just as good if not better than they're doing it. This experience should be invaluable because you get to see how they handle everyday problems which you may one day have to handle yourself.

Barber Wisdom

Barber wisdom is acquired through experience and one's genuine love for barbering. If barbering is nothing more than a hustle or just another way to make money to you, barber wisdom will elude you. You will never find it. There are many smart barbers with a knowledge of the craft. They can shave a client and perform all types of hair cutting techniques, but they lack the wisdom to move their craft to a higher level. Deeper than common sense, having wisdom will potentially give you a greater outcome. For instance; a common sense barber may believe that their success comes from how good he or she cuts, how nice the shop is and how cool or how much swag they have. While all of those things may be essential for success, a wise barber understands that it's all about the customer. It's about how good you make the customer feel. You can be a mediocre barber, cutting in a rundown shop and make the customer feel like a million dollars. Wisdom always takes you to another level, so while other barbers are arguing over who's the best, the wisest barbers are busy cutting hair.

Wise barbers are also open to new ideas and better barbering procedures. We're open to it because we're searching for it. It's just that simple, because what we do is a way of life and not just a hustle. When Hustlers put down their clippers at night, they shut off everything barbering. Any ideas that could possibly make their work easier is not even on the radar. Not so for wise barbers. We often leave the shop thinking about how we can do something better or easier. If you feel like this, you're that barber. The barber who really loves this tonsorial occupation.

Wisdom Cuts

I thought I knew the best way until someone showed me a better way. You don't know what you don't know.

When a little boy learns to ride a bike, you will hear him say that he learned to ride all by himself. He will never mention the training wheels, for they gave him support to stay upright when he had none. The training wheels also helped him get from point A to point B, but he will always believe he got there without the help of training wheels.
He will never see the value of the training wheels until he grows up and becomes the training wheels for another boy's bike.

Good followers become good leaders. If you won't follow, you'll never successfully lead.

Some of us miss "it" because of our inability to tell an authentic from a counterfeit. So we hook up with the wrong people, pass up the good deals and make the wrong decisions time after time. Let your next move be the right move, get a mentor.

A young man searching for knowledge finally found the famous wise man that sat around sharing wisdom with all those who would receive it. The young man was taken aback when he entered the wise man's home. The home was a complete mess. There were no lights or running water, roaches and rats ran freely throughout the house. The wise man asked the young man if he came to get wisdom. The young man looked perplexed and asked, "How could you be a wise man and live like this"? The wise man leaned forth and said, "Easy, this is what happens when you don't do what you know to do."

Wherever you are right now in your career, never forget those who helped and mentored you. You might believe now that you would have accomplished the same things without them, but that's not how you felt when you needed their help. Above all, never offer your mentors less than what they offered you. It's better to offer them nothing until you can match or exceed the opportunities they gave to you

Surround yourself with people who give you no choice but to strive for greatness.

You can walk in a successful man's footsteps and still not arrive at the same destination. True success will branch off like a fork in the road and you'll need to have some morals and integrity to know which way to go.

You have a gold mine in your hands, but you don't respect it because you found a flaw in the person that gave it to you. Does that really change the value of what's in your hand? Or are you being psyched out by your thirst to find something better? Don't throw away what's in your hand and allow someone else to pick it up.

There's a difference from someone who shows and someone who shows off. People don't like the show off and if they don't like you, they won't patronize you. Rethink your approach.

Remember those who truly helped you for they are a rare find

When being mentored to success, don't think because you quit, you're finished. Quitting is NOT going to the next level. You've just chosen a new teacher, another route, a different class. Are you wasting time? Only time will tell.

A true level of intelligence for any man or woman is to know that they don't know everything. Only then can new insight and information make its way to you.

Be careful who you allow to whisper into your ear about your present situation. The wrong person could get you to cut off friends and make moves you shouldn't. When the dust clears, the ear whisperer will be gone too.

It's not real, it's a counterfeit. Designed to fool you and knock you out the game, off the job, out of the partnership or maybe out of the relationship. It looks good, taste good and even feels good, but it's a fake! It will leave you looking stupid with nothing if you aren't careful.
Take heed!

It's difficult to teach someone to do something the right way when they're already making money doing it the wrong way.

Before you get caught up with your present day accomplishments and think you're the hottest thing since buttered bread, remember how far you've come in just 5 or 6 years. Then remove everyone out of your life that came into your life during that same period.... Now how hot are you? Stay humble.

Chapter 11 Industry Barbers

After my many years of experience and meeting barbers from all over the country, I've come to the conclusion that there are basically three types of barbers working in the industry today. No barber is better than the other, I just thought I'd share the basic types of barbers in the industry today.

The Neighborhood Barber

The first barber I would like to discuss is the "Neighborhood Barber". The Neighborhood barber is the everyday barber, the average barber. They've chosen barbering as their

Judging At NYC Barber Battle 2012

vocation and they work hard every day to do well enough to take care of their families. Neighborhood barbers don't care about the newest products and barber gadgets on the market today. They're more traditional when it comes to technique and they're not really interested in the fancy gadgets we see today. They laugh at the hair art craze we presently see going on throughout the country and don't consider that barbering at all. They know little or even care about being a celebrity barber or stylist and make all of their money in the shop from their neighborhood. While they may not be up on the latest trends, they do, however, become the staple of the community and are the barbershop owners we see in our communities today.

The Plugged In Barber

The second barber is the "Plugged In Barber". The plugged in barber is the neighborhood barber hooked up to the internet. The social websites on the net has opened up a whole new world for neighborhood barbers. They now see the many opportunities available for a good barber to look into. Plugged-in-barbers go to national events, learn the latest techniques and now see the potential for them to be a barber/educator or even a celebrity barber. Plugged in barbers are on the road more and more, traveling to barber battles and hair shows. They yearn to see their favorite online barber, take a few pictures and chop it up a bit. The plugged in barber is most importantly the gas for the many engines that keep the hair shows and the industry event shows going. They're buying the tickets, the clippers, and the new products we're seeing popping up all over the country. The plugged in barber wants to be the best at what he or she does and is always looking to get some advanced education to help make them better. These barbers are the future and many of them are already making videos and posting them on YouTube and other social websites to be viewed by their fellow barbers. It doesn't take long for them to realize the power of the internet and they will be amazed that hundreds, maybe thousands are now following them seeking to learn what they've been taught.

The Celebrity Barber?

The third barber is the celebrity barber and you may hear that term quite a bit if you attend hair shows and events. Wikipedia says that it's a person who has a prominent profile and commands a great degree of public fascination and influence in day-to-day media. A celebrity has great popularity appeal, prominence in a particular field, and is easily recognized by the general public. That being said, you can be a celebrity in your neighborhood as well. Wherever people recognize you as being a professional in your field and are fascinated by your success that could qualify you as a celebrity. Once a barber reaches this level, he or she will need to decide how they will proceed from that point on. They need to ask themselves; "What do I want to communicate to my fellow barber? Do I want to show or show off"? Before I go any further, let me say this; Every barber has the right to make money the way they want but once they acquire celebrity status they should be careful to do things right.

The celebrity barber must remember that he or she has achieved their success because of the people. No matter how good you are, if people aren't following and patronizing you, your celebrity wouldn't mean anything. Smart celebrity barbers give back by sharing information which will help other barbers. Some things you can give away for free. Most of what I shared on video for free could be readily found in the instruction book. It really doesn't take much to show you appreciate your followers, you just have to have it in your heart to do something for them. Your followers will appreciate your help and continue to support you even more. Be smart and you'll have longevity. This doesn't mean that the barber works for free, it means that the barber gives some of what they have so that others will benefit. I truly believe in being compensated fairly for the work I do and no barber can give back if he or she has nothing to give. Be sure to get your money and know your worth and you will never run short of change yourself.

On the other hand, there are barbers (a very small minority I might add) that exploit the barber community just to make a dollar and they really don't care whether others are helped or advanced by their deeds or not. They will tell lies and make you think they never gave a haircut for less than $50.00. They make videos that show nothing, but their lifestyle and how much money they have. Even with their how to videos, they spend more time showing off than showing. Aside from the moral and ethical ramifications, they will never acquire real celebrity and the money they could have made if they had just done things right. People will acknowledge them, but won't patronize them because they don't want to get burned again. The celebrities' relevance and longevity will be cut off by their own selfish greed.

For example; you could sell some cheap product that doesn't work that well or you could search for one that really works and sell that one instead. What's the difference? The first product doesn't work, so the customers don't come back. The second product works, so the client reorders and you're in business forever. At the end of the day, celebrity barbers who just take and don't care, shorten their success, but celebrity barbers who give their best will have dedicated clients and customers for years to come. Remember this: ***Don't strive to look cool cutting hair, but strive to make hair cutting look cool. That will eventually open doors for you. If you seek to make the industry better, more doors and ideas will open up to you.***

PLATFORM ARTIST

A platform artist is one of the most fascinating jobs in the hair industry. If you love to travel and wouldn't mind hitting the road or airways from coast to coast, a platform artist might be the career for you. Before you get too excited, there are a few things you may need to know. As a platform artist, you are an educator and a salesperson. Your chore is to demonstrate and teach. To show the hair care products and tools in a way that the spectator can identify with them. As an educator, the platform artist uses the stage to demonstrate and explain how to use the tools and products to produce the latest styles. They explain new techniques that show off the product while performing the hair trend. Some areas of platform artistry concentrate on business-building in the hair industry. Trade shows, clipper companies and even beauty schools employ business platform artists to teach people how to sell their products. Having a cosmetology or barbers license is the first step toward ensuring a post as a platform artist. It is important that one be documented to perform the job at hand. Secondly, having your own shop or salon helps when seeking platform artistry. Most companies seek out business owners in the community because they tend to be more sales oriented when doing platform work. You should likewise, have a passion to help and teach others for that is usually the basis for the sale; teaching people how your product will help them work faster, better etc.

Some other important attributes that a good platform artist should possess is the ability to speak well and keep the attention of the audience. There are many good barbers and stylists who are talented when it comes to cutting and styling, but just fall short when they need to communicate to large crowds. If you suffer from stage fright or you have trouble holding the attention of the listener, you might not want to venture into the platform arena. Posessing a strong, charismatic personality is imperative if you want to make it here. Also, when you have some down time you want to brush up on the latest tools and techniques to stay sharp, mentally. Jump at every chance to learn because your knowledge is your credibility. As a platform artist, you are expected to always be at the vanguard of what's happening. Most companies provide educational training of their own where you can attend and take an examination. You must pass this exam to be certified to demonstrate the products and services sold. Once you get pass this hurdle, you could be well on your way. If you're willing to put forth the effort, perseverance and time, you can become one of the leading platform artists and be in great demand. Platform artist can work full time or part time, but most work part time while they work full time in the industry.

As a platform artist, you'll travel frequently to perform at high profile events such as conferences, conventions, hair shows, advanced training centers, corporate events, and any other hair industry function imaginable. Each presentation is different; some presentations are designed to promote a product or a technique and others are designed for the simple purpose of getting others in the industry excited in general. Whatever the case, you could be quite busy if you're good at what you do.

How Do I Get On?

It's good to be known in the industry for the good work you do. Attend hair shows, enter hair battles and showcase your work whenever possible. Utilize your website and social networks to showcase your work. Stay relevant and put out work that helps others. Barbers and stylists usually work at a barber shop or salon for steady income and then work weekends or part time as a platform artist. A platform artist should also demonstrate a professional presence and be comfortable in front of people. Lastly, they must process a type of creativity that draws attention to what they do.

Money

The salary potential for platform artists varies between $600-$800 per day (plus travel expenses) depending on their methodological and presentation skills as well as their status. While the occupation of platform artists is rarely full-time, some top platform artists in the country make an income in the high six-figure range. On the other hand, there are lesser-known artist who make substantially less.

Al's Keys For Barbering Success

- Your goals must be clear and concise. (To the point)
- Identify your strengths and weaknesses (Be honest)
- Work for someone or do an apprenticeship program first even if you have the money   to open your own shop or school.
  Good followers make excellent leaders. People who can't follow make poor leaders.
- Whatever you plan to do, first sit under someone who's doing it. Don't let not being the boss be a problem for you.
- Document your work, your progress. pictures, videos, etc.
- Attend industry functions and network. Don't be annoying. Just introduce yourself and pass on your business card.
- Learn to promote yourself by helping others. Key to good promotions. Try not to be a pest, but make sure you get your message across. Don't spam or bombard people with your message.
- Promote others and doors will open for you.
- Be honest about everything or say nothing.
- Check your character! Your personality is the type of perfume or cologne you wear, your character is how you really smell; shady, sneaky, backstabbers, liars, etc. Don't do well.
- You should have a crazy work ethic!

- Know when to boast and know when to be humble. Show humility most of the time.
- Save your money.
- Be consistent!
- Be where you need to be. Be in the right place.

*Here are some tips for achieving your goals:

- Identify and contact the corporation for which you would like to work with.
- Talk to the representatives at the next trade event you attend.
- Have a resume and portfolio of your work to show off if you get the chance to speak to the right person.
- Demonstrate a charasmatic personality
- Remember that the ability to travel is a requirement. Travel and costs will be covered by your corporation

The Barber Game

This here barber game, No it ain't like rap. Nobody's signing you to multi-million dollar contracts to sell their clippers or push their products. Nobody's waiting to hook you up or put you on. You'll have to do that for yourself. You're working hard trying to prove you're the best and "ain't" nobody really paying for that. ~ Alsmillions

You see, there's nothing wrong with striving to be the best, but you better know the rules and be smart. Every barber you hear that's "doing big things" had to create a market for what he or she is doing. Coming up, I never looked to impress another barber because I knew he wasn't paying me. The clipper companies will never need to spend millions on advertising because they get free promotion from every video, or every photo of a barber holding a pair of clippers.

Now, am I telling you to give up and stop doing these things? Of course not. That's how I made it happen, but I always knew who my target market was. I only catered for the people that would and could pay me. Many of you are showing off and posting pictures for bragging rights alone, but not one dime will come from one barber trying to prove he's better than another barber. I post to impress the people I cut or want to cut and individuals who can benefit from my products.

Know who your target market is so that you don't waste time doing things that don't produce a harvest.

Just a little something else nobody's going to tell you.

#RealBarberTalk

Wisdom Cuts

Get excited about what you do! Especially if you operate in an atmosphere of integrity. Clients and customers are desperate to find a person like you.

If you got it, you got it! You don't have to fake it, make it, or shake it. You just need to show up!

If you finish, you've won!

Don't expect recognition from those who seek to compete with you. Press on, your day will come.

Your strength is in your problems. Your freedom is in your captivity. People become very resourceful when they have their backs up against the wall. You can find freedom a real success when you use your down time to seek answers.

Going to the next level is a gamble. Everybody wants to go, but few people want to assume the risk. They'll say the right things, but all the while they're afraid to make that move. The risk takers will make enemies quick because they remind the safe players they're not where they thought they were. When you truly have something to offer, the odds are in your favor, but you have to know that.

Build your foundation from the stuff people throw at you.

No matter the profession, you're going to see shady behavior. People are jockeying for position, thinking they're better than you and not trying to let you in their clique. So don't go quitting because you were treated a certain way as a barber. Suck it up and get back on your grind, because it is what it is. Black, white, rich, poor, saved, unsaved, gay, straight, male, female, whatever the case. From preachers to barbers, it doesn't really matter. Human nature is basically all the same.

Our focus should not be to do better than this one or that one, but you should be focused to just do better. Your real competition is with yourself!

You can shine without being obnoxious. Carry yourself in a way where people know you're somebody and not get on their nerves.

There's nothing wrong with thinking you're the best, just don't get blown away when you find out you're not.

Chapter 12 Money, Avoiding The Broke Barber Syndrome

Before I became a barber, I was just a customer in the chair and I knew of a condition that seemed to plague barbers everywhere I went. I've met countless barbers who suffer from what I now call the "Broke Barber Syndrome". The Broke Barber Syndrome has been in existence for years, but it came through like a tsunami back in the 80's and 90's. The problem was that, no matter how much money barbers made, they always found a way to end up broke. Crack cocaine was prevalent, and buying questionable merchandise was the way to go. I was just hitting the barber scene and I still had not learned that it's not how much money you make but how much money you bring home. I soon became guilty of this behavior because money and customers seemed

Emptychairitis Tour Flyer 2011

to be plentiful. Most clients got a haircut twice a week and $200.00 - $300.00 a day was nothing to make back then even for the mediocre barbers in the shop. So you ask; how could we be broke when everyone was making money? Well, because everyone was spending money too. From clothes to strippers, that was the barber's vice. Street merchants and crack heads lived in the barbershop because they knew we would buy whatever they had because we acted like we had money to throw away. We bought jewelry, expensive liquor, rims and tires, and all kinds of gadgets. Many of us spend up everything we made during the day, making it rain at the strip club at night. That was the way it was for many barbers back then and that was the thing that kept us broke too.

Oh yeah, we look like we had money, new sneakers, fresh gear with the bling bling and the nice wheels, but for the most part, we were broke. We had a few dollars to pay some small bills, but not enough to pay anything major. We ate chicken wings and fried rice all week and thought we were doing it. We had no money in the bank, our credit was bad, we didn't own any real estate and most of the time, we just had enough to pay booth rent.

Sad, huh? Well, that's the way it was in the nineties and that's the way it still is. The "Broke Barber Syndrome" is alive and well. Barbers are still spending like crazy and putting nothing away for a rainy day. Wanting to open a shop and don't even have a $1000. 00 to get it going.

A barber must be smart with his money. He must learn to put money away and not feel like he or she has to buy or participate in everything that comes up.

I remember this barber's wife coming to the shop to "get the money" from him at about 4:00 every day so he wouldn't spend it. We used to laugh and joke him about it, but I guess he realized that this is what he had to do if he was going to have anything.

One day I figured out that I was spending $300.00 - $400.00 a week "messing" around. I blew almost $15,000.00 eating and buying stuff I didn't even need over a one year period. That's crazy! I could have opened a decent shop with 15 grand. Fortunately, I woke up before it was too late, but how many barbers don't wake up? How many barbers spend everything having a "good time" and never get their acts together.

Don't let the broke barber syndrome happen to you.

Wisdom Cuts

Invest, grind, stack and repeat!

Take your time and plan your strategy. Patience is the key, the money will be there when you're truly ready.

"The rich get richer and the poor get poorer"? Well that's a Kingdom Principle. If you don't use what you have, if you insist on being lazy and slothful, if you continually make excuses as to why you can't do this or that, you will eventually lose everything. God gives every man according to his or her ability. You... Must then invest it wisely, turn it over and show a profit.

Making money and earning money are two different things. Making money is the act of planting the necessary seeds and fertilizer causing your money to grow exponentially. Earning Money is the act of getting paid for every hole you dig or for how long you dig it.

I've come to know that when a person chases money they are not in control, so money comes by chance and or when it's ready. When you master how to position yourself and make yourself attractive enough, the money will come to you.

There is no secret to success, because the secret is out and it's been out for years. We just don't want to do it.

If your main goal is to just fill your pockets, money will come slow to you. Develop a true desire to help others and money will come to you from everywhere.

Barbers! The Tax Man Cometh

Don't skip this section my fellow barbers and stylist, because at the end of the day we all have to pay taxes. As a barber, I found it so hard to keep track of every money transaction I had with all my customers, but I had to work on that like I worked on my fades. Believe me, you do not want to be audited by the IRS. Learn to keep all of your receipts (booth rental, supplies, business related travel, etc.) and keep good records. Get an accountant or good tax preparer to handle your business right. You may not see the benefits now, but when you work off the books, you don't really exist. You can't get a loan without income and tax records. You're not paying into your Social Security and Medicare, so you won't have anything to look forward to when you retire. and besides, not paying taxes is illegal.

First of all, you're responsible for keeping a record and paying the taxes on each client you perform a hair service on. The best way to do it is to keep records of all of your income (including tips) and your expenses like booth rental and supplies. If you have, then this won't be real hard. If you haven't, you'll have a problem and will have to try to reconstruct the year. Then turn this information over to your accountant and let them take care of the rest. Despite what you might think the Internal Revenue Services can really be a big help to you when it comes to write-offs and taxable income. The IRS allows self-employed barbers and stylists to claim deductions, or "write-offs." You see, write-offs decrease the amount of taxable income a hair professional earns each year. Your expenses must be common in the industry to qualify and necessary for your business.

Here are the expenses you can write-off:

*Operating Expenses - Barbers and stylists can write off any and all expenses required to run their business. This includes advertising, purchasing equipment, liability insurance, cleaning supplies, business cards, booth space and uniforms. You can even write-off the dry cleaning expenses.

*Education & Licensing fees You can only write off barber school expenses if you are single and earning less than $80,000 - $160,000 annually. Now if you're married filing a joint return, your school write-offs may include tuition only, and not textbooks.   Want to get your master barber license? You can also write off licensing fees and continuing education expenses. This includes the cost for the courses, as well as any expenses incurred while taking the courses, such as transportation, meals and lodging.

*Miscellaneous Expenses - If a barber or hair stylist is a member of a professional organization that requires membership dues, the amount paid is tax-deductible. If they subscribe to a trade magazine, the subscription fee is also deductible. The hair professional can deduct other miscellaneous expenses, such as money spent towards customer gifts, refreshments, attending conferences and hair shows.

*Write Off Forms - To write off your barber expenses, you must complete IRS Form 1040. Enter your business expenses in the 1040's "Deductions" section. You can take a standard deduction if your total expenses do not exceed the set dollar amount allowed. If your expenses are more than the standard deduction dollar amount, you need to select itemized deductions. By doing this, you are able to list your expenses item by item. To do itemized deductions, attach IRS Form 1040 Schedule C to your regular 1040. *Reference: Faizah Imani, Tax Write-Offs For Barbers, Small Business. Chron*

I know this might seem like a lot to remember, but it's better that you take the time now to do things right than to mess around and get audited for not paying your taxes. Get yourself an accountant and have them set up a plan for you. You'll need to keep all of your payment receipts (rent receipts, bills, etc.) Also called accounts payable. Then give that to your accountant along with your sales receipts (haircuts, products sales, facials, etc.) Also called accounts receivables. Most accountants will set you up to pay your taxes quarterly. Once your system is set up you're just have to focus on bringing back the receipts.

If you're a barber or stylist working a new start up, you can probably do this yourself. Larger businesses will probably want to consult an accountant to advise you what to do. Whatever the case, make sure you do it.

Chapter 13 Partnership?

A partnership is the relationship existing between two or more persons that come together to carry on a trade or business. Each person contributes money, property, labor or skill, and expects to share in the profits and losses of the business.

So now that you really know what a partnership is, I can't begin to express to you how important it is for you to choose the right person as your partner. Take your time with this process and don't proceed based on your feelings alone. Your financial future and peace of mind is at stake, so do your due diligence before going forward.

You should not consider partnering with someone simply because you need more money. Chances are, you'll probably choose the first person who has the money and that could be the wrong person. You'll do better to wait until you can secure the money necessary to go forth. If you decide to move forward with a partner, be sure to vet them. Do you know someone (other than your spouse) whom you really trust with your money and future to go into business with? I mean, that's the question you must ask yourself when considering a partnership. Can I trust this person(s) to do right by me if we go into business together? If you can't honestly answer that question in the affirmative, then you should not consider that partnership. Just because both of you work in the same industry and have the same desires for success, doesn't mean that you should be partners. In my own experiences, I always find that a partner is lacking something that's important to the success of the partnership. They either have the money, but not the work ethic necessary to help make it happen or they're broke and don't have the work ethic. Either way you might not want that individual for a partner. Let's say the both of you have the money needed and good work ethic, but your visions are different. You should not enter into a partnership until you guys are on the same page when it comes to where you want to go with the business. There should be complete transparency when it comes to bills and important business matters.

Make sure your potential partner is not envious or jealous of you and is morally and ethically sound as it relates to social and business matters. You'll need to spend some time with them before you could know these things, so if you're saying: "How could I know that"? That means you just haven't spent enough time with them yet. Trust me, this is very important to know. Don't ignore questionable behavior going into the partnership, because this could be a sign of things to come. Take note of how your potential partner treats and talks about their friends and previous business associates. This will give you a good idea of how you'll be treated if things get rough. You don't want to be partners with someone who has no problem cheating, lying or even talking about you to others. This type of behavior could cause things to get really ugly, so don't just partner with someone without first considering the character of the person.

Another thing you should consider before entering a partnership is that you are personally responsible for your partner's liabilities related to the business. One partner can take actions - such as signing a contract - that legally bind the partnership entity, even if all the partners were not consulted. Each partner is also personally liable for injuries caused by one partner on company business. In other words, say one partner almost slices off a client's ear while cutting hair, all partnership assets, as well as each partner's personal assets, are at risk. Of course, a partnership can protect itself against such risks by carrying the proper insurance.

Disadvantages of a General Partnership:

- Partners may have different visions or goals for the business.
- There may be an unequal commitment in terms of time and finances.
- There may also be personal disputes.
- Partners are personally liable for business debts and liabilities.
- Each partner may be liable for debts incurred, decisions made, and actions taken by the other partner or partners.
- At some time, there most certainly will be disagreements in management plans, operational procedures, and future vision for the business.
- You may encounter difficulty in attracting investors.

For these and other reasons, general partnership agreements should be drawn up carefully with legal counsel, and signed by all partners. Additionally, there should be a means in place of dissolving the partnership in the case of death, disability, or if one partner should want out of the business for any other reason, personal or professional. General partnerships can be less expensive and require less paperwork and formalities than a corporation, but the partnership agreement is a key element and should be drawn up with due diligence on the part of all parties.

Advantages of a General Partnership:

- You have a shared financial commitment.
- You can pool resources, expertise, and strengths.
- There is a limited start up costs.
- There are few formalities (mostly applicable licenses).

General partnerships can thrive when each partner brings a specific strength to the business. If each partner takes on a defined role and there is general agreement on the business plan, goals, and visions from the outset, a partnership can be advantageous. Work can get done more quickly, and having several partners involved will increase the potential of acquiring resources and attracting backers. In the end, the success of such an endeavor depends largely on the personalities of the parties involved.

If you Decide on a Business Partnership

You should create a "business prenup" that will protect a business if someone leaves.

This "business prenup" should spell out what will happen to your company if a co-owner:
- Wants out of the business
- Wants to retire
- Goes through personal bankruptcy
- Wants to sell his shares to someone else
- Goes through a divorce
- Passes away

You have two choices: you can have a business attorney write up your partnership agreement or you can do it yourself. If you decide to do it yourself, a good choice is "Business Buyout Agreements", which walks you through the creation of a legal contract — a sort of "premarital agreement" for your business — that protects everyone's interests. This document will help ensure a smooth transition following someone's departure.

Wisdom Cuts

You can't get in the way of a man and his dream. No matter what you may want to happen, if it runs contrary to what he wants, there will be a problem.

Some people would rather drown than to be saved by the rope you're holding.
P.S. And that's OK!

So they're not treating you like you expected? You're spending your days trying to figure out what you've done to get the cold shoulder. You feel used and unappreciated because what you've done has seemingly gone unnoticed. They paid you to do what you did. If you did anything extra, that's on you. That's the chance you take. That's your gamble! It might pay off and it might not. If you don't get the pat on the back, the bonus, the accolades or even a phone call, you now know how to play the game better and one day you're going to win.

When people think they "know" you, sometimes they don't respect or believe what you have to say no matter what your expertise might be. You can get offended, but get over it, you've got work to do.

Separate yourself from negative people. Remember, everyone can't go with you and those that can't, don't want you to go either.

Once people "think" they know you they no longer respect your advice. They dismiss your advice as if it doesn't work and you are just making stuff up. The next man can come by and say the same thing you said and they act like God himself said it. Don't get mad, it's just human nature.

Don't allow your life to be connected to people who don't really believe in your vision, but hang on "just in case". They only hamper your success. It may be hard, some feelings may be hurt, but at the end of the day.... You need to get rid of the dead weight!

Don't let them talk you out of what's best for you!

Chapter 14 Last Words

Family First

I know you've been taught to work hard and sacrifice to get to where you want to be, but in all of your endeavor, don't forget family. When I say family, I mean the spouse and kids. Even if you don't have kids, you'll have to make time to spend with your spouse. Don't take them for granted, he or she will understand why you're always working long hours. Yes, you need the money, but you'll have to organize your day so you won't have to work late and leave early for work in the morning. I'm telling you from experience, a few months of that will destroy any good relationship.

You see, your spouse loves you and understands there are bills due but they also need you. They need to know that you still love them, they need to hear that there's no one else and they need to see you making time to be with them. Too much time away from each other is unhealthy for the relationship and will cause resentment and arguments. If both spouses work and you guys never have time for each other, it can open the door for someone else and neither of you want that. If there are kids involved, make time for them, even if you have to bring them to work and take them out after work, but make sure you let them know you love and appreciate them. You're their parent and you're all they've got. Kids just want to spend time with you and they really don't care what you're doing as long as you're doing it with them.

Don't make the mistake so many people make. They work hard for years sacrificing everything, even their families and when the marriage breaks up, they don't understand what happened. Whatever you starve, will die. If you don't feed your marriage and family, it will die.

Wisdom Cuts

If you starve something long enough, it will eventually die. That includes addictions and relationships. Sometimes we feed our careers more than we feed our relationships and the relationship dies. In your quest for financial success, make sure you keep your priorities straight when it comes to family or you just might cause the relationships between you and the ones you love to die.

You'll never have to worry about your resources when your relationship with the source is in good standings.

You might be a step slower, and a few pounds heavier. You might even have a few lines in your face and grey hairs popping up everywhere, but you know you still got it. Do what you want and need to do to feel better, but don't let anyone break your spirit. Maintain your purpose, your reason for doing what you do. Don't stress over someone else's success but rejoice for them, because your day is still coming. Above all, stay the course; don't get off track because your time is now!

You must have purpose. When you lose your purpose, you shorten your days on this earth.

Life is a series of test. You'll know you've failed the test when nothing in your life changes.

Are you waiting for an apology when the one that offended you has gone on about their business? You need to forgive them and let that go. Why forgive? Forgiveness frees you from the psychological bondage of that person. Anger kills you slowly in every way and you don't want to give someone else that much power over you. People ruin their lives and embarrass themselves because they can't let it go. Move on! You got things to do, money to make.

It's what you believe that works for you. Your belief system has taken you to your present place.

Humbling Experience

The Young Men At Silver Oak Academy

Throughout the latter part of my barbering career I always tried to remain humble no matter how great the achievements or the amount of money I've made. I never let my so-called "celebrity" in the hair industry go to my head. Now there might be some that will disagree, because I had to change how I dealt with them, but deep down they know I'm the same guy. In March of 2015, I began working as a teacher at Silver Oak Academy in Keymar, MD. Silver Oak is a high school for young men who've had some run-ins with the law. The courts try to give these young men another chance to get the education and personal life in order by sending them to Silver Oak Academy. The young men are given the opportunity to get their high school diploma or GED and take workforce classes to give them a viable trade. They can get everything from OSHA certifications to culinary and barber training.

Over the last year I've had the opportunity to work as the master barber/ teacher at Silver Oak Academy. This experience was unlike any teaching function I've ever had. I was not ready for what I signed up for initially, but looking at what I gained, I thank God for every moment. I was always used to people being opened to what I had to say, because for the most part they had to pay to hear what I had to say. I was not prepared to have people disrespect me in my face. To hear a young man the age of my son tell me how he was going to "kick my ass" as soon as he could get the chance. Yes, I'll admit I took my tie off a few times and told them to bring it, but Silver Oak showed me how what these boys were saying and doing shouldn't be taken personal. They were hurting, so they lashed out because they needed somebody to show them that they really cared. When I got that, everything changed. My relationship with these young men got better practically over-night and I was no longer wanting to quit. My personal life got better on every level because I no longer took things personal. This new mind set was supported by a book I read called; The Four Agreements, by Don Miguel Ruiz. A must read for everyone, especially teens. It talks about how important your word is and how you should not assume anything. It also teaches you not to take anything personally and to always do your best. These four agreements will change how you do business, how you interact with friends and family and above all keep you drama free!

Today, I'm not the same "Alsmillions" you've seen on YouTube and at hair shows. I'm a better man. Not perfect, but better and I hope you've gained some information, acquired some tools to help you do what you're doing better. All the best to everyone of you and I'll see you at the top!

My Objective Was To Share With You Wisdom....... Without The Pain